raw cookies

raw cookies

60 Delicious, Gluten-Free Superfood Treats

Julia Corbett

North Atlantic Books
Berkeley, California

Published by
North Atlantic Books
P.O. Box 12327
Berkeley, California 94712

Cover and interior photography by Julia Corbett
Cover and book design by Claudia Smelser
Printed in the United States of America

Raw Cookies: 60 Delicious, Gluten-Free Superfood Treats is sponsored and published by the Society for the Study of Native Arts and Sciences (dba North Atlantic Books), an educational nonprofit based in Berkeley, California, that collaborates with partners to develop cross-cultural perspectives, nurture holistic views of art, science, the humanities, and healing, and seed personal and global transformation by publishing work on the relationship of body, spirit, and nature.

North Atlantic Books' publications are available through most bookstores. For further information, visit our website at www.northatlanticbooks.com or call 800-733-3000.

Library of Congress Cataloging-in-Publication Data

Corbett, Julia, 1983-
  Raw cookies : 60 delicious, gluten-free superfood treats / Julia Corbett.
     pages   cm
  ISBN 978-1-58394-821-7
  1. Cookies. 2. Raw foods. 3. Cooking (Nuts) 4. Cooking (Fruit)
5. Gluten-free diet—Recipes. I. Title.
  TX772.C65924 2014
  641.86'54—dc23
                                    2014006895

1 2 3 4 5 6 7 8 9 UNITED 19 18 17 16 15 14

Printed on recycled paper

contents

cacao-based cookies

nut-based cookies

seed-based cookies

raw butter cookies

fruit-based cookies

167   frostings

introduction

I feel most free when I am creating, sharing, and letting inspiration flow through me. I witnessed this happening with friends I met in Hawaii. I experienced a life-changing moment when I stepped foot on the islands, for the first time being in this place without the framework of a "vacation." I was part of a team, making delicious raw foods for a group of retreat guests, and meeting so many new and wonderful people along the way. One particular event had me working alongside an expert in the raw foods field, Melissa Mango, at a permaculture retreat led by Bruce Horowitz. I got to harvest fresh island wild foods and fruits, and incorporate them into the food we were making. I was drinking fresh cacao smoothies for breakfast, and I learned how to open wild young coconuts. There were also many edible flowers to make the food beautiful. It truly was paradise.

Eventually, I found the confidence inside to make one of my raw pies. At this time, I had been making them for only a short while, and I felt I was still learning to master this art. After the retreat was over, many of the organizers, volunteers, and guests stayed a bit longer to build community and continue to work on the land planting trees and clearing space for the new retreat center. I decided to make one of my pies with a farmer's market pineapple and some cacao. The pie turned out amazingly delicious and was enjoyed by my new friends. I knew this was something I had to continue doing—making raw desserts and sharing with those around me—as a way to open up and be myself. Making this type of food inspires creativity so naturally, since it utilizes the most unique foods and flavors. It brings you closer to nature, discovering foods in your local ecosystem, and beyond, without the use of chemicals and overmechanized processes. It's so full of joy!

My first Hawaiian raw pie, made with fresh pineapple and cacao, decorated with a hibiscus flower.

There is an abundance of fresh coconuts on the Hawaiian Islands, and often there are coconut stands off the side of the road. Here, a stand in Kauai offers fresh young, sprouted, and mature coconuts.

My Story

Growing up, my sister and I would always tag along with my dad for our weekly grocery shopping trip to Port Townsend, a charming Victorian seaport in Washington State. We would scour the aisles for our favorite foods, excitedly asking our dad if we could have this or that, usually sweet things such as those little pocket fruit pies and mini doughnuts. One stop I always loved at the grocery store was the bakery and the cookie counter. When my sister and I arrived, the bakers knew us by name since we were frequent visitors. Every time we went there, we would each get a day-old cookie, ones that were frosted with bright colors or speckled with sprinkles, and we would gobble them down with huge smiles on our faces. This must be when I got hooked on cookies.

Through meditation, yoga, and a local food co-op I found in college, I was able to ease myself into a more organic and whole foods lifestyle. I loved eating a fresh scone after a long run, and I couldn't get enough rice crispy treats as a quick snack to fuel my intense exercise. The co-op had the best baked goods, by far, and was using all organic, unrefined ingredients, a new concept for me. The experience inspired me to think about how delicious healthy food could actually taste, especially the raspberry oat breakfast bars! These were my fuel for yoga class, and my whole outlook on how I should live my life changed drastically during that time.

In 2005 I let go of gluten-containing products, out of necessity, when I began seeing a naturopath who woke me up to the realization that these foods were really causing harm in my body. Gluten-free products were still pretty new to the natural foods world. Luckily I was living in Seattle, Washington, when I discovered a bakery with gluten-free sweets called Flying Apron. They had the most amazing maple shortbread, and I splurged on a mini pumpkin pie. I revisited Flying Apron many times, and they always had new daily treats, including cake, pie, cookies, bars, and anything else a lover of sweet baked goods could desire. The mini pecan pies were out of this world, and they even had some of those raspberry oat bars, gluten-free style. That got me thinking: why can't I make healthy, gluten-free sweets, too?

About a year later I actually started to make my own raw food desserts. This was less intimidating than baking to me, and more uniquely creative. Making raw pies was my first attempt at creating a unique raw dessert recipe, filled with rich creaminess, and no heavy feeling after I ate it. A raw pie is essentially a cookie crust with a creamy pudding filling. It felt so natural to be making these desserts, and I loved making them beautiful too, since they were made to be shared. My family truly enjoys these treats, and I couldn't be happier that they are now incorporating many of these foods into their daily life. A little raw chocolate or coconut shortbread will easily do the trick!

In 2009 I serendipitously met my now-husband, Brian, and began creating herbal superfood honey mixtures, raw pies, and cookies made with heirloom cacao, all by using superfood ingredients that the company he worked for manufactured and distributed. I couldn't get enough, and soon after I was inspired by Brian to put one of my best herbal honey mixtures into a jar to sell to friends and at small events. This was the beginning of my raw dessert company Diviana Alchemy. People started to rave about the herbal honey product, Diviana Nectar, so I continued to make more and have the opportunities to share it with more and more people. I have slowly grown the product line over the years to contain some of my favorite cookies and chocolates, including Lucuma Cookie Bites and the Nectar Bar, as a small business owner, somewhere I never in the past would have envisioned myself. It continues to challenge me and inspire creativity, and what I love most of all is sharing these magical treats with you! The recipes in this book are made to open the flower of creativity within, and I hope it is enjoyed and shared with much joy!

Raw Cookie Making

Raw cookies are one of the easiest sweet recipes to make. All you need is a food processor, some creativity, and high-quality ingredients to make delicious food. There is room to play with raw cookies, and you can use sweeteners like raw honey or dried fruit to bind the cookies and any combination of nuts and seeds you like. With the right proportions in mind, you're on your way to being a master raw cookie maker.

You can create numerous different textures, like a creamy and dry short-bread, a chunky crunchy cluster, a chewy sweet cookie, and so much more. I like to use coconut flakes in a majority of my cookie recipes, to keep down costs and to create a crumbly texture that is light and more easily digestible. For me, making sweets that taste good is just as important as feeling good from my food, so I create recipes that support this.

The recipes in this book will help you create a foundation for making cookies, pie crusts, and more, with ideas on flavor combinations that work great and support an energetic and healthy lifestyle. Many of the cookies last more than a month if kept in the refrigerator, so you can make a large batch and have them on hand for a super nutritious treat.

What do cookies have that we desire? Sweetness, delicate texture, bold flavors, and you eat them with your fingers! Cookies are fun. I have a desire to make cookies due to all these reasons and more! I want them to be full of healthy ingredients that nourish the body and leave the mind clear. Sweet treats should be health-giving, something that adds to our experience in life, on a balanced and whole level.

So that we are not diminished by what we put into our bodies, I choose quality ingredients that are mineral-rich and grown in soil that is full of life. These ingredients are the foundation of what we create as a recipe, the art we eat.

Every recipe I devise is a reflection of my understanding of the way food works, in my body, in the ecosystem, and in art. The flavors and textures are inspired by the ingredients, which play off each other and mingle into a whole. There is also visual appeal: does it look as delicious as it tastes? We eat with our eyes first. There is a satisfaction in eating something that is full of beauty.

Chocolate Chaga Peppermint Wafers.

What, truly, are quality ingredients? They are often locally sourced or grown on small farms. Whether from near or far, the sourcing matters on many levels. One is for flavor. I want the best and most complex flavor that a particular food has to offer. It must be grown with care, in healthy soils, and with clean water. Then there is the integrity of the farm: where is it located and how are these people being rewarded for their efforts? Because of all the hard work they do, I think farmers should live comfortably. And how is it processed? What type of facility is being used and is it well maintained? What type of equipment is used in processing? Ideally, there will be minimal processing involved in getting ingredients to the table. Obviously we can't know every step of the process completely, but do your best to learn how products are made, and ask questions of your local farmers when possible.

When preparing food into deliciousness, we want to respect the process it has taken to get to edible form. I love to use whole ingredients, combined together with my own energy to make wonderful, handmade sweets.

In addition, I want to make it clear that in these recipes there are some unique and sometimes difficult-to-find ingredients, but you can still make the cookie recipe. Just omit the dry ingredients that you don't have, such as herbs or superfoods, and replace them with something you do have that complements the flavors in the recipe, like extra lucuma or maca powder. Don't feel as if you need to have all the ingredients used in this book to make super delicious raw cookies. The ingredients that you love will shine through. Enjoy the inspiration!

Organic, Local, Wild, and Heirloom

I make an effort to find the best ingredients available, wherever I am. These include organic, locally grown, wild, and heirloom varieties. The ingredients used in this book are completely organic, local, or wild sourced. Some are heirloom or wild, from around the world and grown in pristine environments. Others are local and organic, found in farmer's markets and natural grocery stores.

The reasons for sourcing the best ingredients are many. Fresh and organic ingredients, grown in proper soil, will provide the most dense nutrition, with the vitamins and minerals your body needs for optimal functioning. Supporting small farmers and companies with integrity helps to improve

Cacao sprout.

Cacao pods on the tree.

local economies and culture. In addition, well-sourced ingredients tend to have the best flavor, so you can make the most delicious food.

Here is a short breakdown of these categories:

Organic This is food grown without the use of pesticides or unnatural fertilizers. It can be grown as large-scale mechanized agriculture, so always ask if possible. Small farms tend to provide the best organic foods, with attention to soil quality, water source, and high-quality seeds.

Locally grown This term is loosely used to describe where food is grown. Locally grown usually means that the food has been grown within your local ecosystem, has not traveled too far to get to your plate, and is more likely to be fresh.

Wild This can describe the variety of the food, like wild blueberries, or mean that the food was actually grown in the wild, without the use of mechanized agricultural methods. For instance, the nutritional content of a wild blueberry from a pristine mountainside will be different from the nutritional content of a wild blueberry variety grown on a farm. Herbs are more often seen in this category, since they are more likely to be original varieties of a plant, nonhybridized by modern agriculture.

Heirloom The actual seed of a plant can be heirloom if it has been untouched by modern technological hybridization, and the plant must be open-pollinated. Hand selection is considered heirloom, as seed-saving practices may determine the varieties that produce the best yield or have a specific flavor. These are cultivated foods.

Essential Tools for Raw Cookie Making

THE FOOD PROCESSOR

If you can master the tools you use to make recipes, you can make anything. Understanding the way the food processor breaks down ingredients will help you make any cookie you desire. This comes with experience and attention. Here are some tips:

- I like to add my nuts to the food processor first, break them down into a flour-like consistency, and then add the remaining ingredients. If you want textural elements in your cookies, add them right at the end of processing, or even afterward, mixing by hand.

- Raw honey varies greatly in flavor and texture. Depending on the freshness and variety of honey, some are solidified, some super liquid. More solid, or crystallized, honey will sometimes stick in the food processor, so adding too much at once can make the blade seize. Add small amounts if using a solidified honey. Using a liquid honey will help to bind the ingredients in the food processor, but the recipe may require a little more stickiness, by adding dried fruits or coconut butter.

- Dried fruits that are not fresh, but too hard, may not process the way you like, so always try to use the freshest ingredients you can find.

A VITAMIX OR OTHER HIGH-POWER BLENDER

If you want to use a Vitamix or other high-power blender to process your cookies, this can be done easily. The nuts or seeds should be broken down into a flour by blending them in the dry blending container of a Vitamix; blending them in the regular container will also work but may not break down every nut evenly. Using 1–3 cups of nuts is the best amount to blend to get everything mixed evenly into a flour.

Then add everything to a mixing bowl. The dry ingredients should be mixed first to incorporate them evenly. Then add the wet ingredients, like honey, and mix with a fork or with your hands.

If the mixture is too dry, add some honey or a touch of pure water. If the mixture is too wet, add some more nut flour or other superfoods. Then roll the cookies or press the mixture into a pan.

These cookies have great texture, since you turn the nuts or seeds into a fine flour, then can add different textures like chopped nuts or dried fruit pieces. The textural elements of a food-processor-made nut flour and a high-power-blender-made flour are quite different and will affect the end product. I suggest trying out each process and using the type of flours you like most.

Nuts that work best for blending into a fine flour, because of their lower oil content, include almonds, cashews, and hazelnuts.

Here are the different textural elements of almonds: whole soaked, dried, and peeled almonds on top; food-processor-made almond flour on the right; and high-power-blender-made almond flour on the left.

Nuts that work best in a food processor, because of their higher oil content, include coconuts, walnuts, pecans, macadamias, jungle peanuts, and Brazil nuts.

OTHER COOKIE-MAKING TOOLS

Shallow sheet pan, ideally with 90 degree corners (I like Parrish Magic Line pans.)

Brownie pan or square glass dish: 8 × 8-inch with square corners is best

Parchment paper: unbleached, naturally coated

Spatula: wood or other

Wooden spoons

Glass bowls: large and small

Sharp knife

Rolling pin

Pretty serving plates

Cookie cutters

Frosting pen or pastry bag

Food dehydrator or oven

Coffee grinder or spice grinder

Double boiler

TOOLS FOR ROLLING DOUGH

Parchment paper

Rolling pin or straight-sided glass (a drinking glass with straight edges and no handle or ridges)

Cutting board or heavy-duty cookie sheet (a flat surface that can be moved to the refrigerator easily for chilling). If using a cookie sheet, after chilling, move to a cutting board to cut shapes with a knife or cookie cutter.

The dough we work with in raw cookie making is a bit more crumbly than traditional cookie dough. It does not stick together as easily, but must be rolled a certain way to stay in one piece. Here is my technique for rolling dough.

I like to use parchment paper and a French rolling pin or a straight-sided glass cup or jar to roll my cookies, so that I can cut circles or other fun shapes to make cookies that will stick together without using fillers, rather than simply always rolling balls or cutting bars.

Start with two large sheets of parchment paper, say 11 × 17-inch or so, on a flat surface like a cookie sheet or cutting board that can be placed in your refrigerator. Place the dough on top of one sheet, form it into a square by hand, and lightly press it together to make the rolling easier. Fold the edges of the parchment paper over the dough so the dough is enclosed, top with the other sheet of parchment paper, if needed, and flip over with the cutting board or cookie sheet onto another flat surface so it will stay folded like a wrapped present. Folding the parchment paper over the dough is optional, but I highly recommend it, since it will help everything compact together better. Then roll the dough with the rolling pin or a straight-sided glass. You must chill the dough for about 1 hour on a cutting board before cutting, so that the shapes will stick together properly.

Rolling Cookie Balls

If choosing to roll cookies into 1-inch balls instead of rolling the dough flat, keep in mind that many of the recipes in this book use a combination of coconut flakes and honey without a sticky binder like dates, which may take some practice to compact together easily. If needed, some of the honey in a recipe can be substituted with dates, about 1 tablespoon honey per 2–3 dates since the dates are generally drier than honey. When rolling by hand, shaping the dough into a ball first is important, using your palms to cup and shape the dough into a ball, or by using your fingers. Rolling between the palms of your hands in a circular motion is what will shape the dough into nice, even, and smooth-surfaced cookies.

Ingredients

NUTS AND SEEDS

These highly nutritive foods are filled with vitamins and minerals, each with its own special properties. These nutrients include magnesium, zinc, selenium, and copper, minerals that are sometimes deficient in Western diets. Nuts and seeds are also high in antioxidants, phytochemicals, and flavonoids, all known to promote good health.

Often, raw recipes will call for sprouted and dehydrated nuts and seeds; this is the ideal form to use in all the cookie recipes in this book, since soaking will reduce phytic acid, a compound that inhibits some mineral uptake in the body. Most nuts require 2–8 hours of soaking (use pure filtered water or spring water), depending on the nut, in a glass jar or bowl. I generally don't soak macadamia nuts, but it can be done if desired. If you like, also sprout the nuts after soaking and draining, by rinsing the nuts thoroughly, then placing in a colander sitting over a bowl to let any extra liquid drip off, covering with a thin towel or cheesecloth, and letting them sit out overnight or until you see a little tail forming (only certain nuts and seeds will sprout a tail). After soaking, you must dry the nuts before using in most of the cookie recipes—using a dehydrator is best. Dry at around 115° for 18–24 hours or so, until crunchy.

Keep in mind, if you aren't able to soak and dehydrate your nuts, that is okay. Just use dry nuts that are high quality and preferably organic or locally grown. In combination with coconut flakes, the amount of nuts used in many of these recipes isn't high in quantity. With coconut as a

Almonds (raw and unpasteurized): 8–12 hours; can form a tiny sprout

Walnuts: 4–6 hours

Pecans: 4–6 hours

Hazelnuts: 6–8 hours

Jungle peanuts: 4–6 hours; can form a sprout tail

Brazil nuts: 2–4 hours

Macadamia nuts: 2–4 hours, or no soaking

Cashews: 2–4 hours

Pumpkin seeds: 2–4 hours

Sunflower seeds: 2–4 hours; can form a sprout tail

Hemp seeds: no soaking

Sesame seeds: no soaking

Chia seeds: 30 minutes for a gel, or no soaking

major ingredient, I find these cookies to be more easily digestible than many other raw dessert recipes and products available today.

I also call for lightly roasted jungle peanuts in certain recipes, where the nuts will be baked in an oven at around 225° for 20–30 minutes, depending on your oven and the desired darkness of the roast. Personally, I like to roast lightly, so that the skins of the jungle peanuts are just beginning to split, and there is a very light roasted color to the nuts, not dark. Lightly roasting this nut (technically a legume) is recommended because jungle peanuts have a grassy flavor that isn't necessarily pleasant when eaten as a cookie or in a dessert recipe, and sprouting the nut will remove some of this flavor, but the traditional flavor of peanut butter is created only by roasting the nuts. This step is completely optional.

Substituting Nuts and Seeds

If a recipe calls for a certain nut, say almonds, another nut or seed can be used in its place. Remember the oil content of nuts will vary, so using a dry nut, like an almond, will substitute well for hazelnuts, cashews, pumpkin seeds, and sunflower seeds. More oily nuts, like walnuts, will substitute well for pecans, macadamias, Brazil nuts, and jungle peanuts. Coconut usually has no substitutes, however, because coconut will hold the cookie together when chilled. The flavor of each recipe will vary greatly depending on the type of nut used, so the recipes in this book are calibrated to the ingredients listed, and should be adjusted accordingly if you choose to use different nuts. I highly recommend playing around, making your own fun creations and experimentations—don't be afraid to try!

COCONUT

Often coconut is thought of as a nut, but it's actually a fruit or drupe, not a true nut. Coconut is a foundational ingredient for many of the recipes in this book. With a light buttery flavor, delicate texture, and saturated fat content that helps cookies harden when chilled, coconut is the perfect ingredient for raw desserts. Coconut comes in multiple forms, including coconut flakes, coconut butter, coconut oil, and coconut flour. I recommend having them all on hand for making raw dessert recipes, as they are generally more cost effective than other raw ingredients, and highly beneficial to your health. Coconut is high in saturated fats, mostly medium-chain fatty acids, including lauric acid, which are excellent for heart health, metabolism, and lubrication in the body. When using raw fats, all the beneficial nutrients are retained and their structure remains intact. Raw coconut is one of the most healthful fats to consume, and that's only one reason why I love to use it in so many recipes.

Coconut flakes These are dried mature coconut pieces, with nothing removed. Using a fine-cut or macaroon-cut coconut flake is recommended for all recipes here, unless the wide-cut coconut flake is desired for garnish or texture.

Coconut butter This is made from coconut flakes by grinding down dried mature coconut into a liquid paste. Or make your own coconut butter with coconut flakes and a high-power blender (see Coconut Butter recipe on page 19). Coconut butter is rich and creamy, with a density that gives cookies and bars a buttery, hardened quality.

Coconut oil This is the fat that has been removed from the fiber of coconut flakes. Look for virgin coconut oil, which is processed at low temperatures and is a higher quality. Coconut oil will help set creams with a silky texture and is great for making frostings. Coconut oil will be used in both solid and liquid (melted) forms in the recipes. Generally, liquid (melted) coconut oil will distribute more evenly in a dough, and melts at around 76°. Solidified coconut oil is best used in frostings that will be whipped into a buttercream-like texture. Either way the coconut oil is used, it will harden when chilled and helps the contents of the recipe hold together without being baked or dehydrated, as will the use of coconut flakes or coconut butter.

Coconut flour The fiber left behind when making coconut oil is called coconut flour. This ingredient is great for giving a cooked cookie quality to a recipe, but will also dry it out; therefore, adding more oil or oily nuts is required when using coconut flour.

Always buy honey that is raw and unfiltered, meaning it has not gone through any heat processing but has just been centrifuged to get the honey out of the comb, or has simply dripped out of the honeycomb. This is very important to preserve the enzymes present in the honey and the full nutrition of this magical food. If possible, know your beekeeper, or become one yourself! Then you can ask the important questions: Has the honey been processed correctly to preserve the integrity of the product? Has the honey been harvested sustainably by the beekeeper? Bees are an integral part of our ecosystem and our food chain—support practices that support the bees!

Here are the types of honey used in this book:

Crystallized Honey that sits and has not been heat-treated will crystallize over time. This honey has many different textures—some are very smooth with small crystals, and some are more chunky with large crystals. Crystallized honey is great for making cookies because it is thick.

Liquid When honey comes straight out of the hive, it is runny and liquid since it is fresh. The water has not yet crystallized the honey, and this honey is great for blending, for teas, and for making hand-mixed cookies.

Light/white This refers to the color and variety. Very sweet, frosting-like, floral, and citrus flavors are common. Clover, starthistle, and sage are all light honey varieties.

Dark This refers to the color and variety. Dark honey is rich, full-bodied, and flavor-filled with tones of molasses. Wildflower, avocado, and buckwheat are all dark honey varieties.

Brazilian sage honey

crystallized wildflower honey

white clover honey

California sage honey

coastal wildflower honey

Wildflower This is my go-to honey. The flavor is usually well rounded with floral notes and richness. Its flavor will vary depending on where you live, and will be specific to the flowers that grow in your area if you are using a local honey.

My favorites: wildflower honey, starthistle honey, and sage honey.

OTHER SWEETENERS

Stevia leaf powder This no-calorie sweetener is a green herb that will grow just about anywhere, much like culinary herbs. Stevia is a great alternative to traditional sweeteners if you have any sensitivity to sugar. Combining stevia with other sweeteners can create a great flavor. Alternatively, you can use a stevia extract, which is more highly concentrated and should be organically processed.

Coconut nectar Liquid coconut nectar, the sap that comes from coconut palm blossoms, is a sweet liquid syrup that is evaporated through a low-temperature process to make a thick nectar as the final product. This nectar has a lower glycemic index than other sugars and has a rich, full-bodied flavor. Use coconut nectar as an alternative to raw honey when desired.

Maple syrup Grade B maple syrup is higher in mineral content than grade A. This sweetener is not raw but is rich with distinct flavors, like vanilla and toffee. It is very liquid, so it can affect the consistency differently than honey or a dried sweetener does.

Coconut sugar Coconut sugar is made from the coconut palm, using a similar process as with coconut nectar, only evaporated further to create sugar crystals. This sugar has hints of molasses and caramel and has a lower glycemic index than some other sweeteners. Coconut sugar is a good choice for recipes that call for a dry sugar.

makes about ¾ cup liquid extract

½ ounce stevia leaf, dried, or use fresh

¾ cup organic vodka, or enough to cover the stevia leaf

Combine the stevia leaf and the vodka in a glass jar, and steep for 24 hours. Strain the stevia herb with a fine-mesh strainer or cheesecloth to remove all the herb. Store in a small jar, ideally one with a dropper, to be able to use a few drops at a time for a recipe.

Note: In my experience, this stevia extract isn't as sweet as store-bought versions, so when using your homemade version in recipes, try doubling the amount.

Sun-dried cane juice crystals This specific type of cane sugar is not refined; the cane juice is dried by the sun and dehydrated, and retains all the precious nutrients and minerals inherent in sugarcane juice. The texture is somewhat moist, and sun-dried cane juice crystals affect the blood sugar less than any white, refined sugar.

Dates Dates are a natural fruit sweetener, coming straight from the date palm. If possible, find dates that are not heat processed; any variety will do. Date season is in the fall and winter, so they are freshest then. Dates create a nice, sticky texture in desserts and are great for helping to hold a cookie together, providing sweet caramel flavors. I like using a combination of dates and another sweetener for lightness, and for more flaky textures. Always pit your dates!

Cacao Raw 100 percent Arriba cacao, the variety I personally use in my recipes, is an Ecuadorian variety of the cacao plant that has a complex, creamy, delicate flavor with floral notes. Arriba cacao is an heirloom variety of cacao; it is mostly wild harvested and some is small-farm produced. Cacao is rich in antioxidants, magnesium, and bliss-inducing chemicals. Look for raw cacao that is nonhybridized and is grown in mineral-rich soils in a clean environment. The forms of cacao available as ingredients are: cacao beans, cacao nibs, cacao paste, cacao powder, and cacao butter.

Lucuma Lucuma is a fruit from South America that has a bright yellow-orange flesh and a creamy, maple-like flavor. Creamy and sweet, this superfood powder is a wonderful addition to any cookie recipe. This is my favorite superfood! Lucuma is rich in niacin, iron, beta-carotene, and fiber and has a low glycemic index.

Maca This root from high in the Andes mountains has a rich, malty flavor and many nutritional attributes. This adaptogenic food is used to help the body adapt to stress, balance hormones, and boost immunity. Use the powdered form in raw cookie recipes. The flavor of white maca is great for raw desserts.

Mesquite This is a sweet and delicious, protein-packed superfood coming from the pod of the mesquite tree. Mesquite is a great addition to anything with chocolate and can be used as a flour for making cookies. This pod is very rich in the amino acid lysine.

Camu camu Tangy and sour, the camu camu fruit has one of the highest amounts of vitamin C of any food. Camu camu provides a nice balance to sweet desserts and heightens the flavors with a small amount. For use in raw cookie recipes, its powder form is best.

Incan spirulina   Rich in chlorophyll and phycocyanins, spirulina is a green algae full of nutrition. It has a protein content of over 65 percent and has a savory and dense flavor. Spirulina has a great flavor when added to sweet foods and doesn't overpower the other flavors in your recipe when used in the correct quantities.

Jungle peanuts   An heirloom variety of peanuts grown in the Ecuadorian Amazon, jungle peanuts are filled with high-quality fats and protein, are sweet and creamy, and are a great addition to cookies and chocolate. Often, these peanuts are produced in small quantities with better quality control than regular peanuts; thus they tend to be low in aflatoxins or aflatoxin free.

Banana flakes   Heirloom red bananas are used to make this superfood treat. The flakes have a slight crunch, which is a nice texture in cookies, but they also add great flavor to smoothies. Banana powder can also be found. These heirloom bananas are high in potassium, vitamin C, and vitamin B6.

Goldenberries   Also known as the Inca berry, this sweet and tart fruit is bursting with flavor. Look for dark-colored goldenberries for a sweeter flavor. Goldenberries contain high amounts of carotenes and bioflavonoids with great antioxidant power.

OTHER SUPERFOODS

Chlorella   Chlorella is a single-celled algae with high amounts of chlorophyll and protein, and detoxifying properties. The flavor is almost cheesy when combined with oils. Chlorella is great when used with both savory and sweet ingredients like rich nuts and honey.

Chia seeds These tiny seeds are hydrophilic, so they soak up moisture quickly and turn gelatinous to hold ingredients together and create a nice texture. Chia is high in omega-3s and has lots of fiber. Because chia does not have much flavor, it can combine nicely with most other ingredients.

Goji berries An ancient superfood used in traditional Chinese medicine, this berry is filled with essential amino acids, polysaccharides, and antioxidants. Containing many tiny seeds, goji berries are deliciously sweet with a slight bitterness, creating a great superfood that can be used in both sweet and savory dishes.

Tocotrienols Made from rice bran solubles, this delicious powder is high in vitamin E, which is a powerful antioxidant. Look for a high-quality product, like Tocotriene Complex, which also includes rice protein and FOS for a balanced product.

Grassfed whey This supports immune functions and is high in protein. This powder is slightly sweet and creamy, great for making cookies. Always look for a whey powder that is made from grassfed cow's milk or goat's milk, as it will be higher in nutrients, and likely from well-treated animals.

SUPERHERB POWDERS

These ingredients can be hard to find but are worth seeking out. Adding a boost of unique flavors and signatures of herbal medicine to a dessert recipe makes it special, and feels good too. They are optional, though, and all recipes will still work without them.

Hibiscus This flower gives a beautiful, bright pink color to a recipe; it has a tangy flavor and a high vitamin C content. Find hibiscus powder from Mountain

Rose Herbs, online. Substitute with camu camu if you have no hibiscus powder available.

Turmeric This root is used extensively in Indian cuisine with a bright orange color. An extract powder of turmeric is what I use for the greatest potency of anti-inflammatory properties, but the culinary herb powder can be used as well. The flavor of turmeric isn't overpowering, unless too much is used, but will provide a slight root vegetable taste.

Schisandra A berry originating from northeast China and Russia and now also grown in the United States, schisandra is traditionally made into a tea and is considered medicinal. It is a known adaptogen, can be used for many ailments, and maintains healthy cells and energy. Known as a "five flavor" berry, schisandra is complex in flavor and very tart. Use in small amounts, as a powdered extract, in raw cookie recipes.

Ashwagandha An extract from the root of ashwagandha is used in the recipes in this book. This root is used as an adaptogen and for balancing thyroid health. I love the flavor of the extract powder, with bitter caramel notes.

Tulsi/holy basil The extract of holy basil is strong in flavor, so very little should be used in a sweet recipe, but the culinary herb can be used in larger amounts. This herb is high in antioxidants and is also an adaptogen.

Moringa A green herb with an antioxidant punch, moringa is often used as a food, offering a wide array of nutrition, including beta-carotene, vitamin C, iron, potassium, and calcium.

Reishi This medicinal mushroom contains polysaccharides, which help to boost immune function, and is supportive of the liver. As an adaptogen, reishi is known to be a tonic herb that can help cultivate a peaceful spirit. The flavor is rich and coffee-like.

Superfood powders from the right middle, clockwise: ashwagandha extract, schisandra berry extract powder, turmeric powder, mucuna extract, passionflower herb, and chaga extract. In the middle is hibiscus powder.

Chaga This mushroom is used for enhancing immunity, has antiviral properties, and is found growing on birch trees. Beta-glucan, a polysaccharide, provides the potent immune properties in chaga. The flavor is superb for dessert recipes; chaga has a vanilla-like aroma and taste, so it pairs nicely with vanilla bean.

Shilajit This mineral pitch from the Himalayas is super rich in flavor and contains the full spectrum of trace minerals and major dietary minerals. Shilajit contains fulvic acid, which helps to break down calcium deposits. When mixed into recipes, shilajit provides a coffee-like flavor that is pleasantly bitter.

Mucuna An extract of this herb has a robust flavor that pairs well with chocolate. Mucuna is a powerful brain tonic and contains compounds such as L-dopa, which is used by the body to synthesize dopamine in the brain.

These are the most used salts in this book: Himalayan salt (left) and sea salt (right).

Passionflower   This is an herb with calming and sedative properties, containing har-
mala alkaloids, which are MAO inhibitors. The vine of passionflower
is best used as a freeze-dried powder or extract of the stems, leaf, and
flower.

SALTS

Himalayan salt   This is a pink salt from the Himalayas containing all the minerals
needed by the body. The finely ground version is best for raw dessert
recipes.

Sea salt   Any type of sea salt will work, but my favorite is Hawaiian Deep Sea
Salt, with large crystals that can be tasted throughout a recipe in little
bursts of saltiness. Typically, sea salts are coarse ground.

Real Salt   A salt from Utah that has a slight pink color and is unrefined, Real Salt
comes from an ancient deposit of sea salt. Real Salt has a mild flavor
and pairs well with any recipe.

nut butter

Makes about 1–1½ cups nut butter

3–4 cups of your favorite nuts
few pinches of sea salt

Soak and sprout the nuts, by soaking in pure water overnight for most nuts (see Nut Soaking Guidelines on page 17).

Dehydrate the nuts at 115° for at least 6 hours or until crunchy.

Depending on the oil content of the nut, use either a high-power blender for oily nuts (blend for about 1 minute) with the tamper, or a food processor for dry nuts (process for about 5–6 minutes).

If using a blender, place the nuts into the container and start on low, then gradually increase to medium speed. Using a tamper, keep moving the nuts around, and if necessary add a touch of coconut oil or olive oil to keep the nuts moving. Mix until smooth, about 1 minute.

If using a food processor, go straight to mixing, and let it continue for about 5–6 minutes. Mix until smooth, occasionally stopping to scrape the nuts off the side.

Store in a jar or other sealable container, best chilled to maintain freshness.

coconut butter

Place coconut flakes in a high-power blender, like a Vitamix.

Turn on low speed and gradually increase to medium speed.

Using the tamper, keep moving the coconut around, so it doesn't stop in the blender; otherwise, you will have to turn off the blender and move the coconut to the bottom.

Continue to blend on medium, switching to low if necessary, until the coconut starts to liquefy.

Keep blending, up to 30 seconds, to desired consistency. There will be some texture to the coconut butter, but it should be soft.

Pour into a jar or other sealable container. Store at room temperature.

Makes a little more than 1 cup coconut butter

4   cups coconut flakes, macaroon-cut or fine-cut

Liquid coconut butter.

nut milk

There's nothing like milk and cookies! Use cute glass jars to serve your guests or yourself, and make them feel at home. This is a great treat to serve to kids and adults alike. Share this nourishing and filling treat just about anywhere and you will have rave reviews.

Makes about 4 cups nut milk

1 cup nuts, like almonds, soaked 6 hours, or ⅓ cup nut butter* (see page 30)

3 cups pure water

1–2 teaspoons honey, 1–2 teaspoons coconut nectar, or pinch of stevia leaf powder or stevia extract

1 teaspoon vanilla bean powder or cinnamon

pinch of sea salt

Blend all ingredients in a high-power blender for 20–30 seconds until the nuts are broken down and smooth.

Strain the mixture through a nut milk bag (a fine mesh bag) or a large, very-fine-mesh strainer. A smooth and creamy nut milk results!

Chill if desired, and stir to serve. Keeps for 3–5 days, refrigerated.

*If using a nut butter, preferably a sprouted nut butter, there is no need to strain.

Nut milk with Hemp Seed and Coffee Cream Sandwich Cookies and Lemon Poppyseed Coconut Cream Cookies. ▶

coconut-based cookies

Coconut is the major ingredient in these cookies. Its flavor and texture create a crumbly, buttery treat.

Use medium shredded (macaroon-cut) or finely shredded (fine-cut) coconut flakes in these recipes, and look for the unsweetened variety. A coconut that is processed lightly and not toasted should be buttery and sweet tasting, like mature coconut.

Also used are: coconut flour, which is the product left behind when making coconut oil; coconut butter, which is coconut flakes that have been ground into a smooth paste; and coconut oil, which is the fat that has been separated from the coconut fiber.

basic coconut cookies

Use this base recipe to create your own inspired treats with coconut!

Mix the coconut flakes and nuts together in a food processor until a fine flour forms.

Add all remaining ingredients, and mix until combined and sticky like a crumbly dough.

Roll into cookies or use as a base for a cookie bar.

Chill for optimal flavor.

Makes about 16 1-inch cookies

2 cups coconut flakes, fine-cut

½ cup nuts, your choice

¼ cup raw honey, crystallized

2–4 tablespoons superfoods, your choice

¼ teaspoon salt, your choice

spices/herbs, to taste

coconut goji chewies

Makes about 16 1-inch cookies

2   tablespoons coconut oil

2½ cups coconut flakes (see Chef Notes: Coconut Flake Cuts)

¼   cup raw coconut flour

4   tablespoons sprouted organic brown rice protein powder, or other protein powder

handful of goji berries

1   teaspoon vanilla bean powder

¼   teaspoon sea salt or Real Salt

¼   cup raw honey (crystallized), light colored

Liquefy the coconut oil by placing it into a glass jar and setting the jar in hot water, or use a double boiler (see Chef Notes: Using a Double Boiler).

Mix all dry ingredients together in a large bowl.

Add coconut oil and raw honey, and mix by hand for best results.

Roll into balls, or cut into other shapes with a cookie cutter. This batter is really sticky, so wash your hands after rolling every four cookies or so.

Chill for about 1–2 hours, until hardened into a soft cookie. Store chilled.

| chef notes | **using a double boiler** |

A double boiler can be used to melt down solid fats that can liquefy, for ease of blending or adding dry ingredients to re-solidify into a hardened state.

Fill a medium-sized pot with 1–2 inches of water, and place over low heat on a stovetop. Place a larger glass bowl or metal bowl over the pot opening, to cover the opening, but not touch the water below. Always use low heat to ensure that melting ingredients do not overheat. After contents are halfway melted or so, stir consistently until completely melted, and remove from heat.

| chef notes | **coconut flake cuts** |

For variety and texture, macaroon-cut coconut is ideal in this recipe. Combining multiple coconut products creates the ultimate coconut treat. If you desire more crunch, use a handful of coconut ribbons or almonds, and pulse them lightly into the mix for added texture. If you want a creamy texture, use fine-cut coconut flakes and coconut flour, with a little added coconut butter for a truffle-like cookie.

superfood cookies

Makes about 24 1-inch cookies

1   cup nuts or seeds (walnuts or your choice)

½ cup goji berries

2 cups coconut flakes, fine-cut

3–4 medjool dates, pitted, or dried figs

2   tablespoons mesquite pod meal

1   tablespoon maca powder

½ teaspoon reishi extract (optional)

½ teaspoon shilajit (optional)

pinch of cinnamon

pinch of nutmeg

pinch of Himalayan salt

2–3 tablespoons Diviana Nectar (see Chef Notes: Additional Superfood Flavors) or raw honey, liquid or crystallized

Grind nuts and goji berries in a food processor until a fine flour forms.

Add remaining ingredients to a food processor, and mix until combined and sticking together easily between your fingers. It should look like a crumbly dough.

Shape however you desire; I like rolling balls.

Chill for 30 minutes or longer. (Refrigeration is not necessary, but it creates a better texture.)

chef notes	**additional superfood flavors**

Mixing it up with this cookie is easy. Use your favorite superfoods in this recipe to create a unique version that you will love! Here are my favorite ideas:

Lucuma powder + chaga + vanilla

Spirulina + camu camu powder

Goldenberries + cacao powder

Note: Diviana Nectar is a blend I created for my company Diviana Alchemy, as an adaptogenic, superfood-infused supplement to your diet. It can be used anywhere you see honey used: in dessert recipes, in teas, or in smoothies. Purchase at www.divianaalchemy.com.

Ingredients: raw unfiltered honey, virgin coconut oil, ashwagandha, chlorella, mesquite, mucuna, shilajit, vanilla, cordyceps, ho shu wu, maca, noni, reishi, camu camu, turmeric, Himalayan crystal salt, and spices.

Diviana ⚜ Alchemy

Raw & Gluten-free

Diviana Nectar

net wt. 5 oz (147g)

Herbal Infused Honey.   Handmade with Love.   Stir. Eat. Elevate.

coconut macadamia shortbread

Pulse coconut flakes and macadamia nuts in a food processor until a fine flour forms.

Add remaining ingredients, and mix until they combine into a soft, loose dough.

Line an 8 × 8-inch brownie pan with parchment paper, and press the dough into the pan with your hands, then top with another sheet of parchment paper, and roll a straight-sided glass over the top to evenly compact the dough.

Chill for a few hours. Remove from the pan with the parchment paper, place on a cutting board, release the parchment paper, cut into bars, and serve. Store chilled.

Makes 32 1 × 2-inch cookies

2½ cups coconut flakes, fine-cut

¾ cup macadamia nuts

1 tablespoon coconut oil, solid

¼ cup sun-dried cane juice crystals or coconut sugar

¼ cup raw honey, crystallized

few pinches of sea salt

1 teaspoon vanilla powder

vanilla maple crunch bars

Makes about 24 cookies

⅓ cup coconut butter

1½ cups almonds

1 tablespoon lucuma powder

4–5 tablespoons maple syrup

½ cup dates, pitted

½ teaspoon vanilla bean powder

¼ teaspoon sea salt

few pinches of nutmeg powder

few pinches of lemon zest

1 cup sprouted buckwheat

Soften coconut butter by placing jar of coconut butter into a pan filled with hot water, to make it easier to scoop out.

Blend almonds in a high-power blender for a fine flour, or in a food processor for a more coarse texture.

Add all ingredients, except buckwheat, to a food processor, and mix until fully combined and sticking together like a crumbly dough.

Add buckwheat, and pulse a few times to incorporate it into the mixture.

Line an 8 × 8-inch brownie pan with parchment paper, and press the dough into the pan with your hands, then top with another sheet of parchment paper, and roll a straight-sided glass over the top to evenly compact the dough.

Chill for at least 2 hours until set. Remove from the pan, place on a cutting board, and cut into bite-sized pieces. Store chilled.

coconut-based cookies

cherry hibiscus cookie bars

Makes about 24 2 × 4-inch bar cookies

4   cups coconut flakes, macaroon-
    cut or fine-cut

½   cup Brazil nuts or other nut

¼   cup raw honey, crystallized

⅓   cup dates, pitted

¾   cup dried sweet cherries (Bing or
    Rainier), pitted

few pinches of sea salt

1   teaspoon vanilla bean powder

¼   teaspoon shilajit (optional)

2   teaspoons hibiscus powder

Place coconut flakes and Brazil nuts into a food processor, and mix until broken down into a flour.

Add remaining ingredients to the food processor, and mix until they start to form a loose dough. Test the dough between your fingers to see if it sticks together; if it does, then you are ready to roll it into bars. Add more honey if needed.

Roll into a ½-inch-thick dough between two sheets of parchment paper on a cutting board using a straight-sided glass or a rolling pin to evenly compact the dough.

Chill for 1–2 hours, then cut into bars. Store chilled.

coconut-based cookies

banana goji cookie bars

Use the same process as for the Cherry Hibiscus Cookie Bars, page 46.

Use the same process as for the Cherry Hibiscus Cookie Bars, page 46.

Makes about 24 2 × 4-inch bar cookies

3   cups coconut flakes, macaroon-cut or fine-cut

½   cup Brazil nuts or other nut

4–5 tablespoons raw honey, crystallized

⅓   cup dates, pitted

2   tablespoons lucuma powder

¼   cup goji berries

5   tablespoons banana flakes or powder, or ¼ cup dehydrated banana

1   teaspoon camu camu powder

few pinches of sea salt

pinch of cinnamon

lemon poppyseed coconut cream cookies

Makes about 20 1½ × 2-inch cookies

½ cup cashews

2½ cups coconut flakes, macaroon-
cut or fine-cut

1 teaspoon lucuma powder

½ cup dates, pitted

1 teaspoon vanilla bean powder

1 tablespoon poppy seeds

3–4 tablespoons raw honey (liquid or
crystallized) or coconut nectar

pinch of nutmeg

¼ teaspoon lemon zest

¼ teaspoon Himalayan salt

Lemon cream

½ cup coconut oil

2 tablespoons olive oil

4 tablespoons lemon juice

¼ cup sun-dried cane juice crystals
or coconut sugar

1 tablespoon raw honey (liquid or
crystallized) or coconut nectar

¼ cup cashews

¼ cup pure water

⅛ teaspoon turmeric powder

pinch of Himalayan salt

2 tablespoons poppy seeds

Blend cashews in a high-power blender to make a flour.

In a food processor, mix the coconut flakes and cashews until combined.

Add all remaining ingredients to the food processor, and mix until a loose dough forms.

Line an 8 × 8-inch brownie pan with parchment paper, and press the dough into the pan with your hands, then top with another sheet of parchment paper, and roll a straight-sided glass over the top to evenly compact the dough. Remove the parchment paper, and set the pan aside while making Lemon Cream.

For the Lemon Cream: Melt the coconut oil in a glass jar placed in hot water, or over a double boiler (see Chef Notes: Using a Double Boiler on page 38).

Place all ingredients for the Lemon Cream (except poppy seeds) in a high-power blender, coconut oil last, and blend until smooth and creamy. Stir in poppy seeds by hand.

Pour Lemon Cream over the dough, and chill for about 2 hours, until set.

Remove from the pan, place on a cutting board, and cut into squares. Store chilled.

lucuma cookie bites

Makes about 36 1-inch balls

4   cups coconut flakes, macaroon-cut or fine-cut

½   cup Brazil nuts or almonds

⅓   cup dates (optional), pitted

4   tablespoons lucuma powder

1   tablespoon maca powder

¼   cup raw honey, crystallized

¼   teaspoon cinnamon

pinch of fresh grated nutmeg

¼   teaspoon Himalayan salt

Mix coconut flakes and Brazil nuts in a food processor until broken down into a flour.

Add remaining ingredients into the food processor, and mix until sticking together like a loose dough.

Roll dough into 1-inch balls, and chill until ready to serve. Store chilled.

These are two different shape options in making Lucuma Cookie Bites, either rolling 1-inch balls or pressing into bars and cutting into bite-sized pieces.

plum and date coconut bites

Mix coconut flakes and Brazil nuts in a food processor until broken down into a flour.

Add remaining ingredients to the food processor, and mix until combined and a dough has formed.

Roll dough into 1-inch balls, and chill until ready to serve. Store chilled.

Makes about 24 1-inch balls

3 cups coconut flakes, macaroon-cut or fine-cut

¼ cup Brazil nuts or other nut

2 tablespoons coconut butter

½ cup dates, pitted

¼ cup dried plums, chopped

3 tablespoons lucuma powder

few pinches of Himalayan salt

⅛ teaspoon cinnamon

¼ teaspoon vanilla bean powder

cacao-based cookies

One of our favorite foods worldwide, cacao has its origin in Central and South America. The cacao bean holds properties that can alter the mind, sending waves of bliss and transporting us into a world of delight. The addition of sweetness to cacao is relatively new and helps to balance the bitterness present in cacao.

Heirloom wild cacao is my choice ingredient, sourced from Ecuador and grown in high-elevation volcanic soil with rainwater or spring water. Although there are many different types of cacao sourced from many regions around the world, choose a raw cacao that is clean and free from toxins associated with poor handling of the product, as it can contain mycotoxins and mold.

◀ *Cacao pods in Kauai.*

Cacao Varieties

There are four main varieties of cacao: Arriba Nacional, Forastero, Criollo, and Trinitario. For the most flavorful product, use the Arriba Nacional or the Criollo varieties; use Forastero for mild flavoring.

Arriba Nacional An heirloom cacao originating in Ecuador, Arriba Nacional has floral notes and a rich flavor. This cacao is grown on fertile soils with clean water and air at higher than normal elevations. True Arriba Cacao is limited in quantity and has a low yield, but it has wonderful floral flavors with jasmine notes.

Forastero A high-yield cacao variety that has a more buttery chocolate flavor.

Criollo A variety with complex flavors, aroma, and a low yield.

Trinitario A mix of Forastero and Criollo, has a complex flavor and a higher yield.

Hybrid Most of the cacao available today is hybridized. Genetic selection of certain varieties for flavor and yield has been done since ancient times, when the Mayans and other Mesoamericans worshipped this incredible food. Finding nonhybridized cacao is difficult if not impossible, but is highly encouraged so as to preserve the medicinal qualities of this plant. Wild food of any kind is generally superior in nutrition.

Cacao Ingredients

Cacao beans These are the whole form of cacao, coming directly from the cacao pod. The fruit around the cacao bean is removed after a fermentation process that brings out the flavors in cacao. Cacao beans are great to eat alone or with a bit of honey.

Cacao nibs The nibs are simply crushed cacao beans. The cacao beans literally fall apart when you crush them. They are crunchy little bits that add texture to a chocolate recipe.

Cacao paste Creamy and rich, cacao paste is stone-ground cacao beans. When the beans are ground down, they turn into a liquid from the friction and then they solidify into paste when cooled. This can either be melted or be used dry to make either a creamy or a textured cookie.

Cacao powder This is the most commonly found cacao product and is great for adding a chocolate flavor without adding too much fat. The cacao powder is separated from the fat of the cacao bean, or cacao butter. The fat content of cacao powder is usually around 15–20 percent. This powder imparts a rich chocolate flavor to dessert or smoothie recipes, and is an easy-to-use ingredient.

Cacao butter The fat separated from the cacao bean is cacao butter. This doesn't contain many of the nutrients and antioxidants found in whole cacao. It is a great binder in recipes, and helps to form bars when making chocolate treats with cacao powder or paste. Cacao butter is also a great moisturizer to use on the body.

cacao powder

cacao butter

cacao paste

unpeeled
cacao beans

cacao nibs

basic chocolate cookies

Use a combination of different nuts, cacao paste, or cacao beans in this recipe. Pay close attention to the ratio here. More oily nuts or more dry nuts will provide a different texture. This recipe is designed to be a basic chocolate cookie that is balanced, crumbly, chewy, and delicious. Mix it up and enjoy!

Makes about 16 1-inch balls

1   cup coconut flakes, macaroon-cut or fine-cut

1   cup nuts, your choice

¼   cup cacao powder

¼   cup raw honey, crystallized

2–4 tablespoons superfoods, your choice

¼   teaspoon salt, your choice

spices/herbs, to taste

Process the coconut flakes and the nuts in a food processor until combined into a fine flour.

Add all remaining ingredients and mix until combined into a sticky dough.

Roll into balls. Or, for bars, line an 8 × 8-inch brownie pan with parchment paper, and press the dough into the pan with your hands, then top with another sheet of parchment paper, and roll a straight-sided glass over the top to evenly compact the dough. Remove from the pan, place on a cutting board, and cut into bars.

Chill for best flavor.

raw chocolate chips

These raw chocolate chips can be used in any recipe that complements cacao, including cookies, puddings, and pies, and are delicious as an uplifting snack as well.

Melt the cacao paste over a double boiler (see Chef Notes: Using a Double Boiler on page 38).

Grind the cane juice crystals in a coffee grinder or a spice grinder until a powder forms.

Add the cane juice crystals to the chocolate along with the salt, and mix until evenly combined.

Set aside for about 20 minutes or until the consistency is beginning to hold its shape slightly, but so it can still be piped on with a pastry bag or tube, or a squeeze bottle with a small, round tip.

Cover a sheet pan with parchment paper, and place the chocolate into a pastry bag or tube, or a squeeze bottle with a small, round tip. Pipe tiny chocolate chip mounds onto the parchment paper, and chill for 20 minutes or leave out on the counter if the shape is holding very well. After the Raw Chocolate Chips are hard, you can use them in recipes. Store chilled for best results.

Makes about 1 cup chocolate chips

1   cup cacao paste, chopped

¼   cup sun-dried cane juice crystals
     or coconut sugar

pinch of Himalayan salt

cacao reishi cookie bites

Place the coconut flakes and the walnuts in a food processor, and mix until a fine texture forms.

Add remaining ingredients to the food processor, and mix until combined and sticky.

Roll into 1-inch balls, add a dusting of schisandra berry extract powder if desired, and chill before serving for best results. Store chilled.

chef notes	flavor additions

Chaga + vanilla

Ashwagandha + chai spices

Mucuna + shilajit + turmeric

Astragalus + moringa powder + camu camu powder

Makes about 20 1-inch balls

1½ cups coconut flakes, macaroon-cut or fine-cut

1½ cup walnuts

3 tablespoons coconut butter (optional, for more smoothness)

⅓ cup dates, pitted

4–5 tablespoons raw honey (liquid or crystallized) or coconut nectar

2 tablespoons lucuma powder

2 tablespoons maca powder

½ teaspoon reishi extract powder

½ teaspoon ashwagandha extract powder

⅓ cup cacao powder

⅛ teaspoon Himalayan salt

pinch of cinnamon

pinch of nutmeg

schisandra berry extract powder (optional)

vanilla and chocolate stripe shortbread

Makes 32 ¼-inch-thick cookies

Vanilla Layer

¼ cup coconut butter

1½ cups coconut flakes, macaroon-cut or fine-cut

½ cup Brazil nuts

1 teaspoon vanilla bean powder

pinch of Himalayan salt

3 tablespoons raw honey (crystallized), light colored

1 teaspoon maca powder

Chocolate Layer

¼ cup coconut butter

1½ cups coconut flakes, macaroon-cut or fine-cut

½ cup walnuts

¼ cup Brazil nuts

1 teaspoon vanilla bean powder

4 tablespoons raw honey, crystallized

5–6 tablespoons cacao powder or ¼ cup cacao paste

pinch of Himalayan salt

¼ teaspoon cinnamon

¼ teaspoon camu camu (optional)

1 teaspoon maca powder

Process all **Vanilla Layer** ingredients in a food processor until a sticky dough forms, almost like a nut butter.

Roll into a ¼-inch-thick dough between two sheets of parchment paper on a cutting board using a straight-sided glass or a rolling pin to evenly compact the dough.

Chill for 30 minutes.

Process the **Chocolate Layer** ingredients in a food processor until a sticky, thick dough forms.

Roll into a ¼-inch-thick dough between two sheets of parchment paper on a cutting board using a straight-sided glass or a rolling pin to evenly compact the dough.

Chill for 30 minutes.

Cut both layers into equal rectangles, about 2 × 8-inch.

Alternately layer the vanilla and chocolate layers until all layers are used. Using a small sheet of parchment paper, firmly press the layers together with your hands, then gently roll a straight-sided glass or a rolling pin over the dough.

Chill for 1 more hour. On a cutting board, slice (so the layers are showing) into cookies ¼-inch thick. Store chilled.

passion fruit and cacao cookie bars

Makes 36 1-inch-square cookies

Macadamia Almond Lucuma Cookie

2 cups almonds

¼ cup macadamia nuts

¼ cup coconut flakes, macaroon-cut or fine-cut

¼ cup raw honey (liquid or crystallized) or coconut nectar

4 tablespoons lucuma powder

1 teaspoon vanilla bean powder

¼ teaspoon camu camu powder (optional)

few pinches of sea salt

Passion Fruit Coconut Cream

¾ cup coconut butter

¼ cup coconut oil

¼ cup passion fruit pulp or juice

2–3 tablespoons raw honey (liquid or crystallized) or coconut nectar

pinch of sea salt

Place almonds in a high-power blender or a food processor, and mix until a flour forms.

Add remaining **Macadamia Almond Lucuma Cookie** ingredients to a food processor, and mix until a loose dough forms.

Line an 8 × 8-inch brownie pan with parchment paper, and press the dough into the pan with your hands, then top with another sheet of parchment paper, roll a straight-sided glass over the top to evenly compact the dough, and set aside.

Blend all ingredients for the **Passion Fruit Coconut Cream** in a high-power blender until mostly smooth—there may be tiny bits of passion fruit seeds if using the fruit pulp.

Melt the coconut butter and the coconut oil in a glass jar placed into hot water, or over a double boiler (see Chef Notes: Using a Double Boiler on page 38).

Pour Passion Fruit Coconut Cream over the cookie layer, and chill for at least 1–2 hours, until set.

For the Cacao Superfood Later: Melt the cacao paste and coconut oil in a glass bowl over a double boiler (see Chef Notes: Using a Double Boiler on page 38). Take the bowl off the heat just before the paste is completely melted, and continue to stir until fully melted.

Blend cane juice crystals in a high-power blender or a spice grinder until a powder forms.

Mix all ingredients for the Cacao Superfood Layer into the cacao paste, by hand, until smooth.

Pour the Cacao Superfood Layer over the Passion Fruit Coconut Cream layer, and chill for about 1 hour.

Remove from the pan, place on a cutting board, and cut into squares. Store chilled.

Note: Be sure to cut into squares when the Cacao Superfood Layer is just hard enough to slice through, but not completely hardened; otherwise, you may make cracks in the chocolate.

Cacao Superfood Layer

2   cups cacao paste

3   tablespoons coconut oil

⅓ cup sun-dried cane juice crystals
     or coconut sugar

1   tablespoon maca powder

½ teaspoon ashwagandha extract
     powder (optional)

½ teaspoon passionflower extract
     powder (optional)

pinch of sea salt

chef notes	**alternative flavors**

If no passion fruit is available, feel free to substitute your favorite fruit in place of the passion fruit pulp or juice. Strawberries, blueberries, or mango would also be great in this recipe.

passion fruit and cacao cookie bars

chocolate macadamia clusters

Melt cacao paste and coconut oil or cacao butter over a double boiler (see Chef Notes: Using a Double Boiler on page 38).

First add lucuma, spices, and salt and mix into the chocolate, next add the honey and mix, then add the bananas and nuts and mix until combined.

Drop tablespoonfuls onto a sheet pan lined with parchment paper. Reshape if desired.

Chill for at least 30 minutes before serving. Store chilled.

chef notes	**alternative flavors**

Substitute for the banana spears and macadamia nuts:

Raisins + chopped almonds

Chopped dried figs + Brazil nuts

Dried blueberries + chopped cashews

Makes about 12 clusters

¾ cup cacao paste

1   tablespoon coconut oil or cacao butter

1   tablespoon lucuma powder

pinch of cinnamon

pinch of nutmeg

pinch of cayenne

pinch of Himalayan salt

4   tablespoons raw honey, liquid, or coconut nectar

3   dried banana spears, sliced into small pieces

¼ cup macadamia nuts, chopped

chocolate chaga peppermint wafers

Process almonds in a high-power blender or in a food processor to make a fine flour.

Add all ingredients, except honey, to a food processor, process until combined into a fine mixture (about 1 minute), then add honey and mix until sticking together like a crumbly dough.

Roll into a ¼-inch-thick dough between two sheets of parchment paper on a cutting board using a straight-sided glass or a rolling pin to evenly compact the dough.

Chill for 30 minutes or so until set firm.

Cut rounds with a cookie cutter, and remove from parchment paper carefully. Chill until ready to serve. Store chilled.

Mix together all ingredients for the **Peppermint Filling** by hand until whipped and fluffy.

Spread the Peppermint Filling onto each cookie, and sandwich with another. Store chilled.

Makes 8–12 sandwich cookies

1   cup almonds

¼   cup cacao paste, broken up into small pieces

2   drops organic peppermint essential oil

1   teaspoon vanilla bean powder

½   teaspoon chaga extract powder

¼   cup sun-dried cane juice crystals or coconut sugar

pinch of sea salt

3–4 tablespoons raw honey (crystallized) or ⅓ cup dates, pitted

Peppermint Filling

2   tablespoons coconut oil, solid

2   tablespoons raw honey (crystallized), light colored

½   teaspoon vanilla bean powder

1   drop organic peppermint essential oil (food grade)

pinch of sea salt

chocolate cherry fudge brownies

Makes 36 1-inch-square brownies

2   cups cacao paste, broken up into small pieces

¼   cup sun-dried cane juice crystals or coconut sugar

¼   cup lucuma powder

½   cup dried cherries, pitted

¼   cup goji berries

½   teaspoon shilajit

1   teaspoon ashwagandha extract powder (optional)

½   teaspoon mucuna extract powder (optional)

1   tablespoon vanilla bean powder

¼   teaspoon Himalayan salt

¼   cup pecan butter or ½ cup pecans

4   tablespoons raw honey (liquid or crystallized) or coconut nectar

½   cup pecans, chopped (optional)

Mix all ingredients, except pecan butter, honey, and chopped pecans, in a food processor until finely broken down.

Add pecan butter and honey, and pulse until combined into the desired consistency. I like some texture, but broken down well. If you like more texture, add chopped pecans at the end.

Line an 8 × 8-inch brownie pan with parchment paper, and press the dough into the pan with your hands, then top with another sheet of parchment paper, and roll a straight-sided glass over the top to evenly compact the dough.

Chill for about 30 minutes to 1 hour, until set. Remove from the pan, place on a cutting board, and slice into bite-sized pieces. Store chilled.

chef notes	**cacao paste**

Raw cacao that has been stone-ground into a liquid is called cacao paste. (See page 56.) In this recipe, the cacao paste is not melted, so it retains some texture and is less dense. The cacao paste provides a creamy, smooth texture to the brownie, making it almost spongy like a cooked brownie.

pecan fudge caramel bites

Pecan Fudge

1 cup cacao paste

1½ cups pecans

4 tablespoons lucuma powder

2–3 tablespoons sun-dried cane juice crystals or coconut sugar

4 tablespoons raw honey, crystallized

1 teaspoon ashwagandha extract powder

½ teaspoon reishi extract powder

few pinches of Himalayan salt

1 teaspoon vanilla bean powder

pinch of nutmeg

¼ teaspoon cinnamon

Pecan Caramel

2 tablespoons coconut oil

¼ cup raw honey, crystallized

4 tablespoons lucuma powder

few pinches of Himalayan salt

½ cup pecans, chopped or whole

Mix cacao paste and pecans in a food processor until broken down.

Add remaining ingredients to the food processor, and pulse until combined together like a sticky dough.

Line an 8 × 8-inch brownie pan with parchment paper, and press the dough into the pan with your hands, then top with another sheet of parchment paper, and roll a straight-sided glass over the top to evenly compact the dough.

Chill while making **Pecan Caramel.**

Melt coconut oil in a glass jar placed in hot water, or over a double boiler (see Chef Notes: Using a Double Boiler on page 38).

Mix all Pecan Caramel ingredients, except pecans, in a bowl, by hand with a spoon, until combined and looking like a caramel. Or mix in a food processor until combined evenly.

Add pecans, and mix until distributed evenly.

Pour Pecan Caramel over Pecan Fudge, then spread evenly.

Chill for a few hours, then remove from the pan, place on a cutting board, and slice into bite-sized pieces. Store chilled.

dark chocolate cookie fudge

Melt the cacao paste, cacao butter, and coconut oil over a double boiler (see Chef Notes: Using a Double Boiler on page 38).

Add the sugar, lucuma powder, tocotrienols (if using), salt, and cinnamon. Stir until combined.

Add the banana flakes, chopped peanuts, and the almond flour at the end, so everything is easily mixed and evenly distributed.

Pour mixture into a parchment-paper-lined 8 × 8-inch brownie pan. Chill for about 1 hour, until set.

Remove from the pan, place on a cutting board, and cut into pieces. Store chilled.

chef notes	**alternative flavors**

Substitute the following seeds or nuts for the jungle peanuts, and add:

Hemp seeds + chopped banana + vanilla bean, deseeded

Chopped pecans + ashwagandha extract powder + mesquite powder

Chopped pistachios + chopped dried cherries (pitted) + nutmeg

Makes about 32 cookies

½ cup cacao paste

2 tablespoons cacao butter

3 tablespoons coconut oil

5 tablespoons sun-dried cane juice crystals or coconut sugar

3 tablespoons lucuma powder

2 tablespoons tocotrienols (optional)

¼ teaspoon Himalayan salt

¼ teaspoon cinnamon powder

¼ cup banana flakes, or other freeze-dried fruit

¼ cup chopped jungle peanuts or other nuts

1 cup almonds, blended into a flour

chocolate chip cookies

Makes 16 2-inch cookies

2   cups walnuts

¾   cup raw coconut flour

3   tablespoons sun-dried cane juice
    crystals or coconut sugar

2   tablespoons lucuma powder

2   tablespoons grassfed whey
    powder or tocotrienols (optional)

    few pinches of cinnamon powder

1   teaspoon vanilla bean powder

½   teaspoon chaga extract powder

¼   teaspoon Himalayan salt

¼   cup raw honey, crystallized

1   tablespoon coconut oil, solid or
    liquid

¼   cup Raw Chocolate Chips (see
    page 59)

Process the walnuts into a fine flour in a food processor.

Add the coconut flour to the food processor, and mix until combined.

Grind the cane juice crystals in a coffee grinder or a spice grinder until a powder forms.

Add the cane juice powder and all remaining dry ingredients (except Raw Chocolate Chips) to the food processor, and process until combined.

Add the honey and coconut oil, and process until the mixture becomes a loose dough that is starting to come together.

Line an 8 × 8-inch brownie pan with parchment paper, and press the dough into the pan with your hands, then top with another sheet of parchment paper, and roll a straight-sided glass over the top to evenly compact the dough.

Remove the top sheet of parchment paper, then distribute the Raw Chocolate Chips onto the top of the dough, and press lightly. If you like, you can place another sheet of parchment paper on top and evenly press to embed the chocolate chips in the dough.

Chill for about 1 hour, remove from the pan, place on a cutting board, and cut into squares. Store chilled.

chewy chocolate chunk cookies

Blend almonds in a high-power blender or in a food processor to make a flour.

Powder freeze-dried fruit by placing into a spice grinder, and grind until a fine powder forms.

Add all ingredients to a food processor, and mix until incorporated as a dough and chocolate chunks are still in small pieces, or mix by hand.

Shape into cookies by using about 1-inch-round dough and pressing between the palms of your hands.

Store chilled if desired.

Makes about 16 cookies

1   cup almonds

3   tablespoons banana flakes or other freeze-dried fruit

3   tablespoons lucuma powder

3–4 tablespoons raw honey (liquid or crystallized) or coconut nectar

1   tablespoon cacao butter, chopped

¼   teaspoon vanilla bean powder

⅛   teaspoon cinnamon

few pinches of Himalayan salt

¼   cup cacao paste, chopped

chocolate thumbprint cookies

Makes about 16 cookies

2 tablespoons cacao butter (chopped) or coconut oil

1 cup almonds

4 tablespoons chia seeds

3 tablespoons lucuma powder

1 tablespoon maca powder

¼ teaspoon cinnamon powder

2 teaspoons ashwagandha extract powder

few pinches of ginger powder

¼ teaspoon Himalayan salt

1 teaspoon cacao powder

¼ cup raw honey (liquid or crystallized) or coconut nectar

¼ cup cacao paste, melted (optional, for a chocolate-based cookie)

Chocolate Drops

½ cup cacao paste

few pinches of stevia leaf powder or 3–4 tablespoons coconut sugar

½ teaspoon ashwagandha extract powder

1 teaspoon lucuma powder

¼ cup goldenberries or other dried fruit

Melt cacao butter or coconut oil over a double boiler (see Chef Notes: Using a Double Boiler on page 38), or place into a glass jar set in hot water.

Blend almonds in a high-power blender to make a flour.

In a spice grinder, blend 2 tablespoons of the chia seeds into a flour.

Add all cookie ingredients to a large bowl—except honey, cacao butter or coconut oil, and cacao paste—and mix until combined evenly.

Add honey and cacao butter or coconut oil, and mix with your hands to incorporate completely. Optional: Add cacao paste, and mix with a spoon.

Roll into 1-inch balls, and press with your thumb to form an indent for the Chocolate Drops. Set aside while making **Chocolate Drops.**

Melt the cacao paste over a double boiler (see Chef Notes: Using a Double Boiler on page 38).

Add all remaining Chocolate Drops ingredients, except for the goldenberries, and mix together.

Drop ½ teaspoon of the Chocolate Drops into the Chocolate Thumbprint Cookies indents, or until filled but not overflowing.

Top with a goldenberry. Chill for 30 minutes before serving. Store chilled.

black and white chocolate chip cookies

Makes 16 2-inch cookies

Chocolate Cookie Layer

¼ cup cacao paste

2½ cups coconut flakes, fine-cut

½ cup cacao powder

½ cup dates, pitted

¼ cup raw honey, liquid or crystallized

¼ teaspoon sea salt

½ teaspoon vanilla bean powder

½ teaspoon camu camu powder

½ teaspoon ashwagandha extract powder

½ teaspoon chaga extract powder

Coconut Chocolate Chip Cookie Layer

2½ cups coconut flakes, fine-cut

2 tablespoons cacao butter, chopped, or coconut butter

¼ cup raw honey (liquid or crystallized), light colored

½ teaspoon vanilla bean powder

¼ teaspoon sea salt

½ cup Raw Chocolate Chips (see page 59)

In a food processor, break down the cacao paste and the coconut flakes until a flour forms.

Add all remaining ingredients to the food processor, and mix until a loose dough forms.

Line an 8 × 8-inch brownie pan with parchment paper, and press the dough into the pan with your hands, then top with another sheet of parchment paper, and roll a straight-sided glass over the top to evenly compact the dough.

Chill for about 1 hour, until hardened.

Process all ingredients for the **Coconut Chocolate Chip Cookie Layer,** except the Raw Chocolate Chips, in a food processor until a loose dough forms.

Mix in the Raw Chocolate Chips by hand.

Press the Coconut Chocolate Chip Cookie Layer on top of the Chocolate Cookie Layer with your hands, and compact again by using parchment paper and a straight-sided glass.

Chill for about 2 hours, until set.

Remove from the pan, place on a cutting board, and cut into bite-sized cookies. Store chilled.

double chocolate cookies

Makes about 24 ¼-inch-thick cookies

½ cup cacao paste

2 cups almonds

¾ cup raw coconut flour

4 tablespoons cacao powder

2 tablespoons lucuma powder

1 teaspoon ashwagandha extract powder

½ teaspoon chaga extract powder

¼ teaspoon Himalayan salt

½ teaspoon vanilla bean powder

3 tablespoons sun-dried cane juice crystals or coconut sugar

3 tablespoons raw butter or coconut oil, solid

⅓ cup raw honey (liquid or crystallized) or coconut nectar

Blend the cacao paste in a high-power blender into a powder, but do not overblend or it will begin to melt.

Blend the almonds into a flour in a high-power blender or a food processor.

In a food processor, add the cacao paste, almonds, coconut flour, and cacao powder, then mix until evenly incorporated.

Add remaining dry ingredients, and mix in the food processor until incorporated.

Then add the raw butter or coconut oil, and pulse until it is distributed throughout the dough.

Finally, add the raw honey or coconut nectar, and mix until a dough forms.

Roll into a ¼-inch-thick dough between two sheets of parchment paper on a cutting board using a straight-sided glass or a rolling pin. Or line a sheet pan with parchment paper, and press the dough into the pan with your hands, then top with another sheet of parchment paper, and roll a straight-sided glass over the top to evenly compact the dough.

Chill for at least 30 minutes, until stiff, place on a cutting board, and cut out desired shapes.

cacao-based cookies

For the White Chocolate Whey Frosting: In a bowl, mix by hand the raw butter or coconut oil and honey until whipped.

Melt cacao butter over a double boiler (see Chef Notes: Using a Double Boiler on page 38), and mix into butter/honey mixture until incorporated.

Add remaining ingredients for the frosting, and whip with a spoon until fluffy.

Frost cookies with the White Chocolate Whey Frosting, and top with ¼ cup Raw Chocolate Chips (see page 59) if desired. Store chilled.

White Chocolate Whey Frosting

3   tablespoons raw butter or coconut oil, solid

3   tablespoons raw honey (liquid or crystallized), light colored (at room temperature)

2   tablespoons cacao butter

3   tablespoons raw grassfed whey powder or tocotrienols

pinch of vanilla bean powder

pinch of Himalayan salt

vanilla and chocolate cream cookies

Makes about 8–12 sandwich cookies

Raw Chocolate Cream Frosting

3   tablespoons cacao paste

¼   cup coconut oil

½   avocado (approximately ½ cup)

3   tablespoons cacao powder, or I Heart Cacao drinking chocolate

3   tablespoons raw honey, liquid or crystallized

¼   cup pure water

½   teaspoon vanilla bean powder

1   tablespoon sun-dried cane juice crystals or coconut sugar

¼   teaspoon ashwagandha extract powder (optional)

¼   teaspoon mucuna extract powder (optional)

few pinches of sea salt

Melt cacao paste and coconut oil over a double boiler (see Chef Notes: Using a Double Boiler on page 38). Remove from the heat when most of the cacao paste is melted, and continue to stir until fully melted.

Add all ingredients to a high-power blender, adding the cacao paste and coconut oil mixture last, right before blending. Use tamper if necessary to blend smoothly.

Remove Raw Chocolate Cream from blender, and pour into a glass bowl. Chill for at least 1–2 hours, or until set into a frosting.

For the Vanilla Cashew Cookies: Process or blend cashews into a flour in a food processor or high-power blender.

In a spice grinder, blend the chia seeds into a powder.

Melt coconut butter over a double boiler (see Chef Notes: Using a Double Boiler on page 38).

Add all ingredients for the Vanilla Cashew Cookies, except for water, to a food processor or mix by hand in a large bowl, adding water last until the desired consistency is reached.

Roll into a ¼-inch-thick dough between two sheets of parchment paper on a cutting board using a straight-sided glass or a rolling pin to evenly compact the dough. Or line an 8 × 8-inch brownie pan with parchment paper, and press the dough into the pan with your hands, then top with another sheet of parchment paper, and roll a straight-sided glass over the top to evenly compact the dough.

Freeze about 10 minutes or until firm. Cut into shapes with a cookie cutter; I like circles.

Using a spoon or a butter knife, frost with the Raw Chocolate Cream Frosting. Store chilled.

Vanilla Cashew Cookies

½ cup cashews

1 tablespoon chia seeds

¼ cup coconut butter

¾ cup raw coconut flour

¼ cup raw honey (liquid or crystallized), white or light colored

¼ teaspoon sea salt

½ teaspoon vanilla bean powder

1–2 tablespoons pure water or lemon juice

chocolate-topped crunchy peanut cookie bars

Makes 24 1 × 2-inch cookie bars

Coconut Maca Cookies

3   cups coconut flakes, macaroon-
    cut or fine-cut

½   cup green raisins

2   tablespoons maca powder

¼   cup raw honey (liquid or
    crystallized) or coconut nectar

3   tablespoons raw coconut flour

1   tablespoon coconut oil, solid

½   teaspoon vanilla bean powder

¼   teaspoon Himalayan salt

Crunchy Peanut Caramel

½   cup jungle peanut butter

¼   cup lucuma powder

½   cup dates, pitted

¼   cup raw honey (liquid or
    crystallized) or coconut nectar

3   tablespoons coconut oil, solid

½   teaspoon vanilla bean powder

½   teaspoon cinnamon

¼   teaspoon Himalayan salt

¾   cup lightly roasted whole jungle
    peanuts

In a food processor, mix the coconut flakes and the raisins until broken down into a fine flour.

Add all remaining ingredients to the food processor, and mix until a loose dough forms.

Line an 8 × 8-inch brownie pan with parchment paper, and press the dough into the pan with your hands, then top with another sheet of parchment paper, and roll a straight-sided glass over the top to evenly compact the dough.

Set the cookie dough aside while making the Crunchy Peanut Caramel.

Place all ingredients for the **Crunchy Peanut Caramel,** except the whole jungle peanuts, into a food processor.

Mix the caramel until a smooth paste forms, add the whole jungle peanuts, and pulse until the peanuts are broken up a bit.

Spread the Crunchy Peanut Caramel evenly over the Coconut Maca Cookie layer, and set aside.

To make the **Chocolate Layer,** melt cacao paste in a glass bowl over a double boiler (see Chef Notes: Using a Double Boiler on page 38), stirring when it starts to melt. Take it off the heat just before melted, keep stirring until completely smooth, then add coconut oil, mixing until melted.

If using coconut sugar, powder it by blending in a spice grinder; or use a high-power blender to blend and powder 1–2 cups of sugar, and use 3–4 tablespoons.

Add all remaining ingredients for the Chocolate Layer to the bowl of melted cacao paste, and stir until completely smooth.

Pour the Chocolate Layer over the Crunchy Peanut Caramel, and spread evenly.

Tap the pan to get out any air bubbles, and chill for 45 minutes to 1 hour.

Remove from the pan, place on a cutting board, and cut into small squares.

Note: Bars must be cut within about 45 minutes to 1 hour of chilling, so the chocolate is easily cut through and doesn't split with cracks.

Chocolate Layer

½ cup cacao paste

2 tablespoons coconut oil

1 tablespoon cacao powder (optional)

2 tablespoons lucuma powder

3–4 tablespoons sun-dried cane juice crystals or coconut sugar

¼ teaspoon vanilla bean powder

¼ teaspoon mucuna extract powder (optional)

¼ teaspoon passionflower extract powder (optional)

Chocolate-topped crunchy peanut cookie bars, page 88

Cookies and cream chocolate-dipped sandwich (page 92)

cookies and cream chocolate-dipped sandwich

Makes about 32 triangle cookie sandwiches

Chocolate Crust

2   cups coconut flakes, macaroon-cut or fine-cut

½   cup walnuts

⅓   cup dates, pitted

4–5 tablespoons raw honey (liquid or crystallized) or coconut nectar

2   tablespoons lucuma powder

1   tablespoon maca powder

¼   cup plus 2 tablespoons cacao powder

¼   teaspoon Himalayan salt

pinch of cinnamon

pinch of nutmeg

Vanilla Cream

¼   cup coconut butter

2   tablespoons coconut oil

1   cup cashews, soaked for at least 1 hour

2   tablespoons chia seeds

1   cup coconut water or pure water

1   vanilla bean, deseeded, or 1 teaspoon vanilla bean powder

Place coconut flakes and walnuts into a food processor, and mix until a fine texture forms.

Add all remaining Chocolate Crust ingredients, and mix until combined and sticky.

Line an 8 × 8-inch brownie pan with parchment paper, and press half of the Chocolate Crust mixture into the pan with your hands, then top with another sheet of parchment paper, and roll a straight-sided glass over the top to evenly compact the dough. Remove parchment paper from top.

Set aside other half of the Chocolate Crust mixture in a covered bowl.

To make the Vanilla Cream, soften the coconut butter and the coconut oil by placing them into a glass jar in hot water, or melt over a double boiler (see Chef Notes: Using a Double Boiler on page 38).

Place all Vanilla Cream ingredients into a high-power blender, and mix until smooth.

Pour Vanilla Cream over the first layer of the Chocolate Crust, and freeze until hardened (4–6 hours).

Then press the remaining Chocolate Crust over the top to form a sandwich, cover with parchment paper, then roll with a straight-sided glass until even. Remove parchment paper from top.

Freeze for 1 hour more.

Remove from the pan, place on a cutting board, and, with a sharp knife, slice into squares first, then triangles.

Place into the freezer again until the Chocolate Glaze is ready. The bars should be completely hard before dipping into the glaze.

To make the **Chocolate Glaze,** melt the cacao paste and the coconut oil over a double boiler (see Chef Notes: Using a Double Boiler on page 38).

If using coconut sugar, powder it by blending in a spice grinder; or use a high-power blender to blend and powder 1–2 cups of sugar. Use 3 tablespoons for this recipe and reserve the remaining sugar for later use.

Add cane juice crystals or coconut sugar and nutmeg to the melted cacao paste, and mix together.

Dip frozen triangles halfway into the Chocolate Glaze, and let the glaze drip off for a few seconds.

Place onto a pan lined with parchment paper, and freeze.

Take out of the freezer 5–10 minutes before serving. Store frozen, in an airtight container.

¼ cup raw honey (liquid or crystallized) or coconut nectar

pinch of Himalayan salt

Chocolate Glaze

1 cup cacao paste, chopped into small pieces

1 heaping tablespoon coconut oil

3 tablespoons sun-dried cane juice crystals or coconut sugar

pinch of nutmeg

nut-based cookies

Almonds, hazelnuts, pecans, pistachios, and walnuts can all be found domestically, even locally depending upon where you live. I love supporting small farmers who love what they do and who sell direct to customers. Find local nuts at farmer's markets or online for the freshest product. This way, you are supporting these farmers to continue to provide product direct to customers, and giving the farmers maximum profit.

◄ *Heirloom jungle peanuts.*

basic nut cookies

Process the dry nuts in a food processor or blend in a high-power blender for a very fine flour.

Add the oily nuts and dry nuts to a food processor, and mix into a fine flour.

Add all remaining ingredients, and mix until combined and sticky like a crumbly dough. If this dough does not stick together easily, process it more or add more sweetener so it will form a cookie and hold its shape.

Chill for the best flavor and texture.

Makes about 16 1-inch cookies

1 cup dry nuts, like almonds

1 cup oily nuts, like walnuts

¼ cup raw honey, liquid, or other liquid sweetener

2 dates, pitted (for binding)

2–4 tablespoons superfoods, your choice

¼ teaspoon salt, your choice

spices/herbs, to taste

gingerbread cookies

Makes about 16 ¼-inch-thick cookies

1 cup almonds

1½ cups coconut flakes, macaroon-cut or fine-cut

¼ cup sun-dried cane juice crystals or coconut sugar

1–2 tablespoons raw honey (liquid or crystallized) or coconut nectar

1 tablespoon mesquite pod meal

1 teaspoon ginger powder

1 teaspoon coconut oil, solid or liquid

¼ teaspoon clove powder

¼ teaspoon cinnamon powder

½ teaspoon ashwagandha extract powder

¼ teaspoon Himalayan salt

Ginger Spice Frosting

¼ cup coconut oil, solid

3 tablespoons maple syrup

2 tablespoons lucuma powder

½ teaspoon ginger powder

few pinches of Himalayan salt

few pinches of cinnamon powder

few pinches of nutmeg

few pinches of anise powder

Using a high-power blender, grind the almonds and the coconut flakes into a fine flour.

Grind the sugar into a powder in a spice grinder or high-power blender.

Place all ingredients in a food processor, and mix until combined and a dough is forming, sticking together easily.

Form a ball, and press, by hand, onto a parchment-paper-lined cutting board. Roll with a straight-sided glass or a rolling pin, if necessary, until the dough is about ¼-inch thick. Chill for 1 hour or longer.

Then cut out shapes with a cookie cutter, and carefully transfer to a plate. Set aside.

To make the **Ginger Spice Frosting,** be sure your coconut oil is solidified; chill if necessary.

Whip the coconut oil in a small bowl with a spoon until most of the lumps are gone.

Mix in the maple syrup, and whip until creamed together.

Mix in all remaining ingredients, and whip until a smooth frosting consistency forms.

Frost Gingerbread Cookies with a butter knife or a spoon, or pipe on with a pastry bag.

Chill until ready to serve. Store chilled.

nut-based cookies

trail mix cookies

Dice dried mango and banana, and chop walnuts.

In a large glass bowl, toss all ingredients together, except honey and coconut oil.

In a small bowl, mix the honey and coconut oil, by whipping with a spoon or fork.

Add the honey/coconut oil mixture to the large bowl, and mix with a fork or with your hands until completely incorporated. Add a little more honey if needed.

Roll into 1-inch balls, and chill until ready to serve. Store chilled.

chef notes	**alternative flavors**

Use these flavors in place of the dried mango, banana, and jungle peanuts:

Dried chopped pineapple + cacao nibs + chopped macadamias

Dried cherries (pitted) + golden raisins + chopped cashews

Dried chopped apricots + dried chopped figs + chopped pecans

Makes about 20 1-inch cookies

¼ cup dried mango

⅓ cup dried banana

¼ cup walnuts

½ cup jungle peanuts, lightly roasted

¼ cup sunflower seeds

¾ cup raw coconut flour

3 tablespoons Raw Chocolate Chips (see page 59)

2 tablespoons lucuma powder

¼ teaspoon sea salt

¼ teaspoon cinnamon

⅓ cup raw honey (liquid or crystallized) or coconut nectar

⅓ cup coconut oil, solid, or raw butter

hazelnut sugar cookies

Makes about 16 ¼-inch-thick cookies

1–2 tablespoons cacao butter

¾ cup hazelnut butter (see "Nut Butter," page 30)

1 cup raw coconut flour

½ cup sun-dried cane juice crystals or coconut sugar

1–2 tablespoons maple syrup or raw honey, liquid or crystallized

1 tablespoon lucuma powder

1 tablespoon mesquite powder

pinch of nutmeg

pinch of ginger

⅛ teaspoon sea salt

Strawberry Cream Frosting

2 tablespoons cacao butter

¼ cup coconut oil

¼ cup cashews, soaked at least 1 hour

½ cup strawberries

1–2 tablespoons raw honey (liquid or crystallized) or coconut nectar

1 teaspoon lemon juice

few pinches of sea salt

Melt cacao butter over a double boiler (see Chef Notes: Using a Double Boiler on page 38), or by chopping and placing in a glass jar set in hot water until melted.

Place all ingredients into a food processor, and mix until a loose dough forms and sticks together when pressed.

Roll into a ¼-inch-thick dough between two sheets of parchment paper on a cutting board using a straight-sided glass or a rolling pin to evenly compact the dough. Cut shapes with cookie cutters.

To make the **Strawberry Cream Frosting**, melt cacao butter and coconut oil over a double boiler (see Chef Notes: Using a Double Boiler on page 38).

Drain and rinse the cashews.

Place all ingredients in a high-power blender, and mix until smooth.

Chill the frosting for at least 2 hours, until set.

Frost the Hazelnut Sugar Cookies by piping or spreading the frosting, and chill until ready to serve. Store chilled.

brazil nut lucuma caramel

Makes about 24–30 caramel pieces

1   cup raw honey, crystallized
⅓   cup coconut butter
¼   cup lucuma powder
1   tablespoon maca powder
¼   teaspoon Himalayan salt
1   teaspoon vanilla bean powder
½   cup Brazil nuts, chopped

In a food processor, mix all ingredients, except the Brazil nuts. The dough should ball up and become caramel-like.

Remove the mixture from the food processor, and place in a glass bowl.

Add the Brazil nuts and stir in by hand until evenly combined.

Press the mixture between two sheets of parchment paper into a ½-inch-thick caramel, using a straight-sided glass or a rolling pin to evenly distribute the caramel.

Chill for 1 hour or longer on a cutting board, then cut into small, bite-sized pieces. Keep chilled until ready to serve. Store chilled.

pistachio rose honey bites

Makes about 24 1-inch cookie bites

Pistachio Cookies

3 tablespoons coconut butter

¼ cup pistachio butter or 1 cup pistachios

2 tablespoons raw honey, crystallized

2 cardamom pods, seeds only, ground, or ⅛ teaspoon cardamom powder

1 vanilla bean, deseeded, or 1 teaspoon vanilla bean powder

few pinches of Himalayan salt

Rose Coconut Cookies

2 cups coconut flakes, macaroon-cut or fine-cut

3 tablespoons dried wild rose petals or 1 teaspoon rose powder

2 tablespoons coconut butter

3 tablespoons raw honey (crystallized), light colored

few pinches of Himalayan salt

⅛ teaspoon hibiscus powder or ½ teaspoon beet juice

Soften coconut butter by placing coconut butter jar into hot water for about 10 minutes, after which the coconut butter will be easy to scoop out.

Place all ingredients in a food processor, and blend until combined fully.

Roll into balls, shape into squares, or roll like a dough between two sheets of parchment paper on a cutting board using a straight-sided glass or a rolling pin to evenly compact the dough.

Chill for at least 1 hour, until set.

Cut shapes with a cookie cutter if rolled. Store chilled.

To make the **Rose Coconut Cookies,** process the coconut flakes and the dried wild rose petals (if using) in a food processor to break down the petals.

Process all ingredients in a food processor until a dough forms.

Roll into balls, shape into squares, or roll like a dough between two sheets of parchment paper on a cutting board using a straight-sided glass or a rolling pin to evenly compact the dough.

Chill for at least 1 hour, until set.

Cut shapes with a cookie cutter if rolled.

nut-based cookies

Sandwich the Rose Coconut Cookies with the Pistachio Cookies (both types of cookies must be cold) by using a small dab of honey in between, then pressing together firmly. Or serve each type of cookie separately. Store chilled.

chef notes	**edible flowers**

For treats that have just one color, add some edible flowers to the mix by using them as a garnish to pull the recipe to a whole new level. The more interesting and vibrant appearance makes the treat more enticing to eat. Here are some edible flowers that I love to use:

Wild roses	Lavender	Culinary sage flowers
Rosemary flowers	Calendula	Marigold
Pansy	Borage	Lilac

maple walnut shortbread

Makes about 16 sandwich cookies

1   cup almonds for almond flour (if
    dehydrating) or 1 cup brown rice
    flour (if baking)

1½ cups walnuts

¼   cup maple syrup

pinch of sea salt

¼   teaspoon cinnamon

Before making the cookies, set out the raw butter
for the Salted Buttercream Frosting at room
temperature so that it will soften.

Mix almonds in a high-power blender until a flour
forms.

Process walnuts in a food processor until broken
down.

Add remaining ingredients to the food processor,
and mix until a dough forms.

Press the dough on parchment paper with a rolling
pin or a straight-sided glass, and roll to a ¼-inch
thickness.

Cut circles, or other shapes if desired, gently
remove, and place onto parchment-paper-lined
dehydrator sheets.

Dehydrate at 145° for 2 hours, then turn down
to 115° and dehydrate for 8 more hours or until
desired texture is achieved.

If baking with brown rice flour, bake at 275° for 20
minutes or until very lightly browned.

The butter should be soft when you make the **Salted Buttercream Frosting.**

If using coconut sugar, powder it by blending in a spice grinder; or use a high-power blender to blend and powder 1–2 cups of sugar, and use 3 tablespoons.

Combine all ingredients together, and mix vigorously with a spoon until fluffy.

Frost half of the Maple Walnut Shortbread cookies with the Salted Buttercream Frosting, and sandwich each one with another cookie.

Store in an airtight container, and eat within 1 week, or store chilled.

Salted Buttercream Frosting

¼ cup raw butter (soft) or coconut oil (solid)

3 tablespoons sun-dried cane juice crystals or coconut sugar

2–3 tablespoons maple syrup or coconut nectar

1 tablespoon lucuma powder

few pinches of sea salt

few pinches of cinnamon

salted ginger chewies

Makes 32 1 × 2-inch cookies

- ½ cup raw coconut flour
- ¼ cup pecans
- 1 cup walnuts
- 2 tablespoons almond butter or other nut butter
- 3–4 tablespoons raw honey, crystallized
- ¼ cup dates, pitted
- ¼ cup sun-dried cane juice crystals or coconut sugar
- 1 teaspoon ginger powder
- ¼ teaspoon cinnamon
- pinch of fresh grated nutmeg
- ½ teaspoon sea salt

Topping

- ¼ teaspoon sea salt
- 3 tablespoons sun-dried cane juice crystals or coconut sugar

In a food processor, mix the first three ingredients until a flour forms.

Add all remaining ingredients to the food processor, and mix until a wet dough forms.

Roll into cookie balls by taking 1 tablespoon of dough and compacting between your palms, then rolling into balls. Or line an 8 × 8-inch brownie pan with parchment paper, and press the dough into the pan with your hands, then top with another sheet of parchment paper, and roll a straight-sided glass over the top to evenly compact the dough.

Chill for about 30 minutes, place on a cutting board, and cut into squares.

For the Topping: Mix together the sea salt and the sugar.

Dip tops of cookies into Topping, and serve. Store chilled.

chef notes	**flavor additions**
	Chai spices + cacao powder
	Anise + lemon zest
	Kola nut + maca powder

jungle peanut butter cookies

If desired, roast jungle peanuts at 275° for 20–25 minutes.

Skin the jungle peanuts by hand if you want a light-colored dough.

Place all ingredients in a food processor, and mix until a ball forms, or a smooth texture forms.

Roll into 1-inch balls. Chill for at least 30 minutes. Store chilled.

Makes about 20 1-inch cookies

2 cups jungle peanuts, skinned if desired

½ cup coconut butter

2 tablespoons raw honey, crystallized

¼ teaspoon sea salt

1 teaspoon vanilla bean powder

1 tablespoon maca powder

Salted ginger chewies ▼

jungle buckeyes

Makes about 20 1-inch cookies

3 tablespoons cacao butter

4 tablespoons cacao powder (or 1 teaspoon cacao butter with 4 tablespoons cacao paste)

2 tablespoons lucuma powder

pinch of stevia leaf powder or stevia extract (optional)

1 teaspoon raw honey, liquid, or coconut nectar

Jungle Peanut Butter Cookies (recipe on page 111)

Melt cacao butter over a double boiler (see Chef Notes: Using a Double Boiler on page 38).

Mix in the powders. After the mixture is smooth, gently stir in the honey. Make sure the honey isn't too cold, or it will seize the chocolate. It should be fully liquid honey—feel free to heat it very lightly so that the ingredients are all the same temperature.

Dip Jungle Peanut Butter Cookies into the chocolate sauce by placing a toothpick into the cookie and dipping it halfway or so. Place the dipped cookies on a parchment-paper-lined cutting board or cookie sheet.

Allow to cool for a few minutes or until the chocolate sauce starts to harden, and dip again. Place back on the parchment paper.

Chill for 30 minutes or longer before serving. Keep chilled until ready to serve. Store chilled.

nutter butter bar

2 cups jungle peanuts, skinned if desired

4 tablespoons lucuma powder

5 tablespoons sun-dried cane juice crystals or coconut sugar

3 tablespoons tocotrienols or grassfed whey protein powder

1 tablespoon coconut oil, solid or liquid

1 teaspoon vanilla bean powder

¼ teaspoon cinnamon powder

½ teaspoon sea salt

1 cup buckwheat, sprouted and dehydrated

Process all ingredients, except the buckwheat, in a food processor until creamy, about 2–4 minutes. Set aside ½ cup. Store remaining peanut butter mixture in a glass container in the refrigerator.

Mix ½ cup of the jungle peanut butter mixture and 1 cup sprouted and dehydrated buckwheat together by hand until combined evenly to make the Nutter Butter Bars.

Roll into balls. Or, for bars, line an 8 × 8-inch brownie pan with parchment paper, and press the dough into the pan with your hands, then top with another sheet of parchment paper, and roll a straight-sided glass over the top to evenly compact the dough.

Chill for about 1 hour, until set. Take out of the pan, place on a cutting board, and cut into 1-inch to 2-inch pieces.

You can simply eat the Nutter Butter Bars, or dip them in melted chocolate (see Jungle Buckeyes, page 112).

Peanuts are one of my all-time favorite nuts. They are so satisfying and a comfort to eat. The variety of peanut I use is called the jungle peanut, an heirloom variety from South America. One thing I love about this nut is the beauty of its skin, with streaks running down the side and a wonderful maroon color. This unique characteristic shows me that this variety is an heirloom.

The flavor in its raw form is somewhat unpleasant to my taste; it is grassy like a raw legume, which it is. I prefer to use these nuts roasted at a low temperature, to bring out the oils and the familiar flavor of this childhood favorite. I roast them in a glass pan, usually roasting a few pans at a time and spreading the nuts out as one layer, so they all roast evenly. Preheat the oven to 275°, and roast for about 20–25 minutes so they are just starting to split in their skins. Let cool, and create your own Jungle Peanut Butter!

walnut hazelnut honey cookies

Makes about 24 1-inch cookies

1½ cups walnuts

1½ cups hazelnuts

3 tablespoons lucuma powder

2 tablespoons mesquite powder

1 tablespoon maca powder

½ teaspoon cinnamon powder

1 teaspoon vanilla bean powder

¼ teaspoon sea salt

½ cup raw honey (liquid or crystallized) or coconut nectar

Blend walnuts and hazelnuts into a flour in a high-power blender or food processor.

In a large bowl, mix all the dry ingredients until combined evenly.

Add honey to the bowl, and mix until a dough forms.

Roll into balls or make other shapes. Chill, if desired, before serving. Store chilled.

chef notes	recipe additions

This versatile recipe can be combined with other layers to form other dessert bars or pies. Some suggested flavor combinations:

Base cookie layer + Vanilla Cream (see page 92) + raspberry jam

Base cookie layer as a pie crust + plum slices + Blackberry Cream (½ cup blackberries added to Vanilla Cream recipe on page 92)

Base cookie layer as a cobbler + peach slices + blueberries + Vanilla Cream (see page 92)

maple almond blueberry frosted cookies

Makes about 16–20 ¼-inch-thick cookies

Maple Almond Cookies

1 cup almonds

3 tablespoons almond butter

¼ cup sprouted buckwheat flour, or
   ½ cup sprouted buckwheat

¼ cup tocotrienols or grassfed whey
   powder

¼ cup maple syrup

¼ teaspoon sea salt

1 teaspoon vanilla bean powder

pinch of cinnamon

pinch of fresh grated nutmeg

1 teaspoon camu camu powder

1 teaspoon ashwagandha extract
   powder (optional)

1 teaspoon moringa powder
   (optional)

Blend almonds into a flour in a high-power blender or a food processor.

Add all Maple Almond Cookies ingredients to a food processor, and mix until combined into a wet dough.

Roll into a ¼-inch-thick dough between two sheets of parchment paper on a cutting board using a straight-sided glass or a rolling pin to evenly compact the dough.

Blend all **Blueberry Frosting** ingredients in a blender or food processor until mixed into a cream.

Add extra lucuma if needed to emulsify.

Spread Blueberry Frosting onto the Maple Almond Cookies, and chill for about 1 hour, until set.

Cut into squares or other shapes. Store chilled.

Blueberry Frosting

3 tablespoons coconut oil

3 tablespoons raw butter or coconut butter

½ cup wild blueberries

3–4 tablespoons maple syrup

pinch of sea salt

1 tablespoon maca powder

1 tablespoon lucuma powder

seed-based cookies

Seeds like sesame, pumpkin, and hemp have a distinct flavor, and I like to pair them with dried fruits. This helps to mellow out the flavors a bit with the sweetness and provides a thick, sticky texture. Seeds also pair nicely with coconut flakes and sprouted buckwheat, which help to produce a lighter feel to the cookie.

◀ *Styrian pumpkin seeds.*

basic seed cookies

Place all ingredients in a food processor, and mix until combined and sticking together like a dough. Some texture is nice with seed-based cookies, so I don't always process the seeds into a flour first, as with many of the other cookies in this book.

Roll into 1-inch balls. Or, for cookie bars, line an 8 × 8-inch brownie pan with parchment paper, and press the dough into the pan with your hands, then top with another sheet of parchment paper, and roll a straight-sided glass over the top to evenly compact the dough.

Chill until ready to serve. Store chilled.

Makes about 16 cookies

1 cup coconut flakes

½ cup seeds, your choice

3 tablespoons raw honey, liquid or crystallized

¼ cup dried fruit, your choice

¼ teaspoon salt, your choice

spices/herbs, to taste

hemp seed and coffee cream sandwich cookies

Makes about 12 sandwich cookies

Coffee Hemp Cream

½ cup coconut oil

½ cup hemp seeds

¼ cup cold-brewed coffee

⅓ cup sun-dried cane juice crystals or coconut sugar

1 teaspoon vanilla powder

1 tablespoon lucuma powder

2 teaspoons maca powder

½ teaspoon chaga extract (optional)

½ teaspoon mucuna extract powder (optional)

pinch of sea salt

¼ cup pure water

Melt coconut oil over a double boiler (see Chef Notes: Using a Double Boiler on page 38), or in a jar set in hot water.

Place all ingredients for the Coffee Hemp Cream in a high-power blender, and mix until smooth.

Chill the cream in a glass jar or bowl until set, best overnight.

For the Hemp Coconut Cookies: Blend the cashews into a flour in a high-power blender or food processor.

Mix the coconut flour, cashew flour, and macadamia nut butter or coconut oil in a food processor, or mix thoroughly by hand.

Place this mixture and all remaining ingredients for the Hemp Coconut Cookies into a large bowl, and mix by hand until a dough forms.

Roll into a ⅛- to ¼-inch-thick dough between two sheets of parchment paper on a cutting board using a straight-sided glass or a rolling pin to evenly compact the dough.

Cut out circles or other shapes, and place them on dehydrator trays.

Dehydrate at 120° for 6–8 hours, or until desired texture is achieved. Let cool completely before frosting with the Coffee Hemp Cream.

Use a butter knife or a spoon to frost the Hemp Coconut Cookies with the Coffee Hemp Cream.

Roll the sides of each cookie sandwich in hemp seeds. Serve immediately, or chill until ready to serve. Store chilled.

chef notes	**cold-brewed coffee**

Cold-brewed coffee is sometimes used in otherwise raw recipes because the flavor is so unique and delicious, and the cold-water method ensures a lower acidity in the final product. Cold-brewed coffee is made in various ways, usually by soaking roasted coffee grounds in room-temperature or cold water for a long period of time, then removing them from the water. One simple recipe: Combine ½ cup coarsely ground coffee with 3½ cups cold water and let sit in a jar or a French press, chilled, for 24–48 hours. Use the French press or pour through a nut milk bag to strain and keep refrigerated for up to a week.

Hemp Coconut Cookies

½ cup cashews

¾ cup raw coconut flour

¼ cup macadamia nut butter or coconut oil, solid

¼ cup hemp seeds

¼ cup raw honey (liquid or crystallized) or coconut nectar

2 tablespoons sun-dried cane juice crystals or coconut sugar

2 tablespoons chia seeds (plus ½ cup pure water)

2 tablespoons lucuma powder

3 tablespoons banana flakes (optional)

¼ teaspoon cinnamon

few pinches of sea salt

Garnish

⅓ cup hemp seeds

Hemp seed
and coffee cream
sandwich cookies

Ayurvedic sesame treats

ayurvedic sesame treats

Makes about 16 1 × 1½-inch cookies

½ cup sesame tahini

1 cup coconut flakes, macaroon-cut or fine-cut

4 tablespoons raw honey (liquid or crystallized) or coconut nectar

4 tablespoons sun-dried cane juice crystals or coconut sugar

1 teaspoon turmeric powder

1 teaspoon ashwagandha extract powder (optional)

¼ teaspoon shilajit (optional)

½ teaspoon dried, powdered tulsi leaves or holy basil powder (optional)

few pinches of sea salt

½ teaspoon chai spices (I use cardamom, cinnamon, black pepper, clove, and allspice.)

2 tablespoons black sesame seeds, or white sesame if no black sesame is available

Mix tahini, coconut flakes, and honey in a food processor until a ball forms.

Add remaining ingredients to the food processor, except the black sesame seeds, which you will add at the very end and pulse a few times to incorporate.

Roll into a ½-inch-thick dough between two sheets of parchment paper on a cutting board using a straight-sided glass or a rolling pin to evenly compact the dough.

Cut into squares or other shapes with a cookie cutter. Store chilled.

fruity sesame turmeric bites

After processing the dough for the Ayurvedic Sesame Treats, except the black sesame seeds, add all the Fruity Sesame Turmeric Bites ingredients, and process again in the food processor. Add the black sesame seeds at the very end, and pulse a few times to incorporate.

Press into a parchment-paper-lined 8 × 8-inch brownie pan, or roll into a ½-inch-thick dough between two sheets of parchment paper on a cutting board using a straight-sided glass or a rolling pin to evenly compact the dough. (You can also roll the dough into 1-inch balls.)

Chill for 1 hour, then remove from parchment paper, place on a cutting board, and cut into cookie squares. Store chilled.

Makes about 32 1 × 2-inch cookies

All ingredients for Ayurvedic Sesame Treats (page 128) plus:

¼ cup dried cherries, pitted

¼ cup green raisins

1½ cups coconut flakes, macaroon-cut or fine-cut

½ teaspoon cinnamon powder

sunflower chewy sugar cookies

Blend cane juice crystals, dates, and water in a
high-power blender until smooth.

In a bowl, mix all ingredients together thoroughly
with a spoon.

With an ice cream scoop or a tablespoon, scoop out
the mixture onto a dehydrator sheet, then flatten
into thin cookies.

Dehydrate at 145° for about 2 hours, then turn
down to 115° for about 18 hours or until dry and
still slightly pliable. Store in a sealed container.

Makes about 16 cookies

½ cup sun-dried cane juice crystals
   or coconut sugar

½ cup dates, pitted

½ cup pure water

½ teaspoon ginger powder

½ teaspoon ashwagandha extract
   powder

few pinches of Himalayan salt

1 cup sunflower seeds, sprouted
   and dehydrated

2 tablespoons chia seeds

pumpkin seed spumoni

Makes about 24 ¼-inch-thick cookies

Turmeric, Hibiscus, and Spirulina Frosting

½ cup coconut oil, solid

½ cup raw honey, liquid, or coconut nectar

pinch of Himalayan salt

1 teaspoon turmeric powder

1 teaspoon hibiscus powder

1 tablespoon spirulina powder

Spumoni Cookies

⅓ cup dates, pitted

½ cup plus 2 tablespoons Austrian pumpkin seeds, or regular pumpkin seeds

¾ cup coconut flakes, macaroon-cut or fine-cut

few pinches of nutmeg

few pinches of cinnamon

few pinches of sea salt

First, make the three frostings. Blend the coconut oil, honey, and salt in a bowl with a spoon, mixing until fluffy and there are no lumps.

Divide the frosting into three bowls, and add one of the three powders (turmeric, hibiscus, and spirulina) to each bowl. Mix by hand, until incorporated evenly.

Chill the frostings for 30 minutes or longer.

In a food processor, mix all the **Spumoni Cookies** ingredients, except 2 tablespoons pumpkin seeds, into a fine crumble.

Add 2 tablespoons of each frosting to the food processor, and pulse a few times.

Add 2 tablespoons pumpkin seeds to the food processor, and pulse a few times until incorporated.

Roll the Spumoni Cookies dough into 1-inch balls. Or, for cookies, line an 8 × 8-inch brownie pan with parchment paper, and press the dough into the pan with your hands, then top with another sheet of parchment paper, and roll a straight-sided glass over the top to evenly compact the dough.

Chill for about 1 hour, then remove from parchment paper, place on a cutting board, and cut into squares. Store chilled.

raw butter cookies

Raw butter is an unpasteurized butter, made from raw cow's cream. This product is full of nutrition, and high in healthy fats, vitamin A, vitamin E, good cholesterol, and lecithin. These nutrients can be difficult to find in plant foods, so some may find it ideal to include animal products such as raw butter in their diet as a health food.For the highest proportion of nutrients (and for humane reasons—cows are designed to eat grass), use raw butter made with grassfed milk.

◄ *Raw grassfed butter.*

basic raw butter cookies

The key here is to use the right amount of butter—don't use too much, since the flavor can be strong depending on the butter's source. Butter is a great binder and will hold a cookie or frosting together very nicely.

Process the nuts into a flour in a food processor or a high-power blender.

Mix all ingredients by hand or in a food processor until combined and sticking together like a dough.

Roll into balls or cut into other shapes. Chill until ready to serve. Store chilled.

Makes about 12 1-inch cookies

1 cup nuts, your choice

3–4 tablespoons raw butter, unsalted

3–4 tablespoons raw honey, liquid or crystallized

2–4 tablespoons superfoods, your choice

¼ teaspoon salt, your choice

spices/herbs, to taste

raw butter and italian almond cookies

Makes about 32 1 × 2-inch cookies

1½ cups Italian almonds

¾ cup raw coconut flour

⅓ cup raw butter

⅓ cup raw honey (liquid or crystallized) or coconut nectar

2 tablespoons grassfed whey powder or other protein powder

few pinches of sea salt

Fig Paste

1 cup sunflower seeds

1 cup chopped figs (I like the white varieties.)

pinch of sea salt

pinch of cinnamon

½ cup green raisins, or other raisins

Blend 1 cup of the almonds into a flour in a high-power blender.

In a food processor, mix the remaining ½ cup of almonds and the coconut flour until whole almonds are broken down.

Add all remaining cookie ingredients to the food processor, and mix until starting to come together like a crumbly dough.

Line an 8 × 8-inch brownie pan with parchment paper, and press the dough into the pan with your hands, then top with another sheet of parchment paper, and roll a straight-sided glass over the top to evenly compact the dough.

Chill for at least 30 minutes or until set, so the Fig Paste can be pressed on.

For the Fig Paste, process the sunflower seeds into a powder in a food processor.

Add the figs, salt, and cinnamon to the food processor, and mix until a paste forms, or the dough is forming a ball.

Add the green raisins and process until they are chopped into small bits, but so there is some texture.

Press the Fig Paste evenly over the dough.

Frost with White Chocolate Whey Frosting (see page 85), using a spoon or a butter knife.

Chill for another hour or more, until set to desired consistency. Cut into rectangles or squares, and serve. Store chilled.

raw butter thumbprint cookies

Soften coconut butter by placing the jar into hot water for about 10 minutes or until the coconut butter is soft enough to scoop out.

Mix the almonds in a high-power blender or food processor into a flour.

Place all ingredients in a food processor, and mix until combined into a dough consistency.

Roll into 1-inch cookies, and press an indent into each cookie with your thumb or fingers, and flatten cookies on the bottom.

Chill the cookies while making the **Cranberry Frosting.**

Place all ingredients for the Cranberry Frosting in a food processor, and mix until a paste forms.

Spoon the mixture into a pastry bag or a frosting tube, and fill the cookie indents with the frosting.

Chill for 30 minutes or longer. Store chilled.

Makes about 16 cookies

5 tablespoons coconut butter

1 cup almonds

4 tablespoons raw butter

3 tablespoons raw honey (liquid or crystallized) or coconut nectar

5 tablespoons lucuma powder

1 tablespoon maca powder

½ teaspoon amla extract or schisandra berry extract powder (optional)

½ teaspoon cinnamon powder

¼ teaspoon Himalayan salt

1 tablespoon sun-dried cane juice crystals or coconut sugar

Cranberry Frosting

½ cup dried cranberries or dried cherries, pitted

2 tablespoons raw butter

3 tablespoons raw honey (liquid or crystallized) or coconut nectar

½ teaspoon cinnamon powder

raw butter snickerdoodles

Makes about 12 cookies

5   tablespoons raw butter (cold)

¾   cup raw coconut flour

¼   cup raw honey (liquid or
    crystallized), light colored

½   teaspoon vanilla bean powder

2   tablespoons lucuma powder

3   tablespoons sun-dried cane juice
    crystals or coconut sugar

pinch of sea salt

Cinnamon Sugar

1   tablespoon sun-dried cane juice
    crystals or coconut sugar

1   teaspoon cinnamon powder

Cut cold butter into chunks, and add it to a food processor.

Add remaining ingredients to the food processor, and mix by pulsing until a dough forms and all ingredients are incorporated.

For the Cinnamon Sugar, mix together the cane juice crystals and the cinnamon in a small bowl.

Roll the dough into 1-inch balls with your palms. Dip each ball in the Cinnamon Sugar until the whole ball is covered, and set on a plate or a parchment-paper-lined dish. Chill for about 1 hour before serving. Store chilled.

fruit-based cookies

There is nothing more delicious than a wild-picked berry—sweet, juicy, and full of flavor. Combining a wonderful berry treat like this in a raw cookie is even more decadent. It can be taken to a whole new level of yum. I encourage you to utilize the fruit ingredients you have on hand, or go out and find them! This is where local and seasonal cookie treats can shine.

There are so many possibilities here, from dried fruits in the cookie to freshly made jams as a topping. Use the basics from the other cookie recipes here to create your own unique cookie treat, and use fruit as a creative addition to add a little sparkle.

sugar-free goji cookies

In a food processor, mix the Brazil nuts and the coconut butter into a paste.

Blend the goji berries in a coffee grinder or a spice grinder into a powder.

Add all ingredients to the food processor, and mix until combined thoroughly.

Press the dough evenly into a parchment-paper-lined 8 × 8-inch brownie pan, and chill for about 1 hour, until firm.

Cut into shapes. Store chilled.

Makes 32 1 × 2-inch cookies

¾ cup Brazil nuts

2 tablespoons coconut butter

⅓ cup goji berries

1½ cups coconut flakes, macaroon-cut or fine-cut

⅓ cup lucuma powder

¼ cup tocotrienols or grassfed whey powder

1 tablespoon mesquite powder (optional)

1 teaspoon stevia leaf powder

1 teaspoon vanilla bean powder

1 teaspoon moringa powder (optional)

¼ teaspoon sea salt

wild berry jam linzer cookies

Makes about 12 linzer cookies

Strawberry Jelly

½ cup strawberries, chopped

1 tablespoon raw honey (liquid or crystallized) or coconut nectar

3 tablespoons chia seeds

Linzer Cookies

2 cups jungle peanuts, skinned if desired

½ cup coconut butter

2 tablespoons raw honey (liquid or crystallized) or coconut nectar

¼ teaspoon sea salt

1 teaspoon vanilla bean powder

1 tablespoon maca powder

First, make the **Strawberry Jelly.** Mix the strawberries and the honey in a food processor until smooth. Place in a bowl, and stir in chia seeds. Set aside.

If desired, roast the jungle peanuts at 275° for 20–25 minutes. Peanuts can also be sprouted; follow the sprouting directions (see Nut Soaking Guidelines, page 17).

Skin the peanuts by hand if you want a light-colored dough.

Place all the **Linzer Cookie** ingredients into a food processor, and mix until a dough forms.

Roll into a ⅛ to ¼-inch-thick dough between two sheets of parchment paper on a cutting board using a straight-sided glass or a rolling pin to evenly compact the dough.

Cut all the cookies with a cookie cutter; then with half of the cookies, cut out a smaller shape in the center to create a linzer cookie, or use a linzer cookie cutter. Or use a simple cookie cutter and sandwich the cookies.

Line up the solid cookies on a parchment-paper-lined sheet pan.

Drop 1 teaspoon of Strawberry Jelly on the solid cookie, then top with the cookie that has its center cut out.

Chill until ready to serve. Store chilled.

fruit-based cookies

fig butter frosted cookies

Place all the **Honey Butter Frosting** ingredients into a food processor, and mix until soft and silky smooth. Don't overprocess so that the coconut oil and the raw butter are melted, or the frosting may separate.

Or mix by hand, by whipping the coconut oil and the butter in a bowl with a spoon, then adding remaining ingredients, and mixing until smooth.

For the Fig Cookies: Chop the figs into small pieces.

Add all ingredients to a food processor, and mix until a sticky dough forms.

Line an 8 × 8-inch brownie pan with parchment paper, and press the dough into the pan with your hands, then top with another sheet of parchment paper, and roll a straight-sided glass over the top to evenly compact the dough to about ¼-inch to ½-inch thick. Or roll between two sheets of parchment paper on a cutting board using a straight-sided glass or a rolling pin to evenly compact the dough.

Remove the top layer of parchment paper, then frost with the Honey Butter Frosting.

Remove the cookies from the parchment paper, place on a cutting board, and cut into squares. Chill for about 30 minutes, until set. Store chilled.

Makes 36 1-inch cookie squares

Honey Butter Frosting

- 2 tablespoons coconut oil, solid
- 3 tablespoons raw butter or coconut butter (cold)
- 3–4 tablespoons raw honey (liquid or crystallized) or coconut nectar
- 2 tablespoons lucuma powder
- pinch of Real Salt

Fig Cookies

- ⅓ cup dried Calimyrna or Turkish figs (white figs)
- 1½ cups coconut flakes, macaroon-cut or fine-cut
- ¼ cup almond butter
- 2 tablespoons coconut butter
- 3 tablespoons raw honey (liquid or crystallized) or coconut nectar
- 1 tablespoon mesquite pod meal
- ½ teaspoon cinnamon
- ¼ teaspoon sea salt
- 3 tablespoons banana flakes or powder (optional)

banana-filled cashew cookies

Makes about 16 cookies

1¼ cups cashews (to make ¾ cup cashew flour)

3 tablespoons coconut butter

3 tablespoons raw butter, or additional coconut butter

2 tablespoons lucuma powder

4 tablespoons banana powder, or 1 tablespoon maca powder plus 1 tablespoon additional lucuma powder

few pinches of sea salt

¼ teaspoon cinnamon

2 tablespoons raw honey (liquid or crystallized) or coconut nectar

Banana Filling

2–3 dried banana spears

Garnish

2–3 tablespoons banana flakes, or sun-dried cane juice crystals or coconut sugar

Blend whole cashews in a high-power blender to break down into a flour, or in a food processor for a more coarse flour.

Place all cookie ingredients into a food processor, and mix until combined and turning into a crumbly and moist dough.

Remove the dough from the food processor, and place into a bowl.

For the Banana Filling: Slice the banana spears into ½-inch chunks.

Take each banana chunk, place dough around it in your palm, and surround the banana chunk by cupping and pressing the dough in your palm. Roll each cookie ball to make it smooth and uniform.

Roll the cookie balls into the banana flakes and eat! Chill the cookies if you like, but the banana will be more hard and chewy.

chef notes	**flavor additions**

Substitute the banana spears and banana flakes with:

Goldenberries + cacao powder

Dried cherries (pitted) + chopped almonds + sea salt

Dates (pitted) + mesquite powder

spirulina banana bread cookies

Makes 32 1 × 2-inch cookies

3   cups coconut flakes, macaroon-
    cut or fine-cut

½   cup raw coconut flour

3   tablespoons hemp protein
    powder, or other protein powder

2   teaspoons chlorella powder

2   teaspoons Incan spirulina powder

½   cup banana flakes or dried
    banana

¼   cup dates, pitted

¼   cup raw honey (liquid or
    crystallized) or coconut nectar

½   teaspoon sea salt

pinch of cinnamon

In a food processor, mix the first five ingredients until they are mixed evenly into a flour.

Add all remaining ingredients to the food processor, and mix until a dough forms.

Add extra honey for a thicker consistency if desired.

Line an 8 × 8-inch brownie pan with parchment paper, and press the dough into the pan with your hands, then top with another sheet of parchment paper, and roll a straight-sided glass over the top to evenly compact the dough.

Chill for at least 1 hour before cutting. Remove from the pan, place on a cutting board, and cut into squares or other shapes. Store chilled.

chef notes	**incan spirulina nutrition**

Spirulina is abundant in chlorophyll, essential fatty acids, and protein. It contains all the essential amino acids, with over 65 percent protein. Incan spirulina, specifically, has the highest amount of phycocyanin of any spirulina. Phycocyanin is an incredible antioxidant that helps to produce stem cells that develop white and red blood cells in the body. Incan spirulina is grown with glacier water in a closed environment with pure air in Ecuador.

schisandra-frosted almond cookies

Makes about 24 ¼-inch-thick cookies

Schisandra Berry Cream

- ½ cup cashews (soaked 2–4 hours)
- ¼ cup plus 1 tablespoon coconut oil
- ½ cup strawberries, stems removed
- ¼ cup raspberries
- 1 teaspoon schisandra berry extract powder
- 2 tablespoons raw honey (liquid or crystallized) or coconut nectar
- 1 teaspoon lemon juice
- few pinches of sea salt

Almond Maca Cookie

- 2 cups almonds
- ¼ cup coconut flakes, macaroon-cut or fine-cut
- 2 tablespoons chia seeds (ground)
- 2 tablespoons maca powder
- 1 tablespoon lucuma powder
- 1 teaspoon vanilla bean powder
- 3–4 tablespoons raw honey, crystallized
- ¼ teaspoon sea salt
- 2–3 tablespoons pure water

Drain and rinse the soaked cashews.

Soften or melt the coconut oil in a glass jar placed in hot water, or over a double boiler (see Chef Notes: Using a Double Boiler on page 38).

Place all ingredients, adding the coconut oil last (just before blending), into a high-power blender, and mix until smooth, using a tamper if necessary.

Place the Schisandra Berry Cream into a bowl, and chill for a few hours, until set.

For the Almond Maca Cookies: Blend the almonds in a high-power blender to make a fine flour.

Add the remaining Almond Maca Cookie ingredients to the blender, and mix until a crumbly dough forms. (Omit the water if making a refrigerator cookie, and not dehydrating.)

Roll into a ¼-inch-thick dough between two sheets of parchment paper on a cutting board using a straight-sided glass or a rolling pin to evenly compact the dough.

Cut into fun shapes with a knife or a cookie cutter.

Place on dehydrator sheets, and dry at 145° for 2 hours, then lower the temperature to 115° for another 6–8 hours or until the desired consistency is reached (or simply chill the cookies until hardened).

When the cookies are cooled completely, frost with the Schisandra Berry Cream just before serving.

lemon cream sandwich cookies

Melt the coconut oil in a glass jar placed in hot water, or over a double boiler (see Chef Notes: Using a Double Boiler on page 38).

Blend all **Lemon Macadamia Cream** ingredients in a high-power blender until smooth and creamy.

Pour into a bowl, and chill for about 2 hours, until set into a frosting consistency.

Blend the almonds in a high-power blender or with a food processor into a flour.

Add all the **Almond Lemon Cookies** ingredients to a food processor, and mix until a loose dough forms, or mix by hand.

Roll into a ¼-inch-thick dough between two sheets of parchment paper on a cutting board using a straight-sided glass or a rolling pin to evenly compact the dough.

Chill for about 30 minutes, until hardened a bit.

Cut into little shapes with a cookie cutter or into circles, and chill until ready to frost.

Frost the cookies by sandwiching two Almond Lemon Cookies with about 1 teaspoon of Lemon Macadamia Cream frosting. Store chilled.

Makes about 18 1-inch sandwich cookies

Lemon Macadamia Cream

3   tablespoons coconut oil
¼   cup macadamia nuts or cashews
3   tablespoons lemon juice
3   tablespoons pure water
1   tablespoon raw honey (liquid or crystallized) or coconut nectar
1   teaspoon lucuma powder
¼   teaspoon lemon zest
⅛   teaspoon turmeric powder
pinch of sea salt

Almond Lemon Cookies

2   cups almonds
3   tablespoons raw coconut flour
2   tablespoons coconut butter
1   tablespoon coconut oil, solid or liquid
3   tablespoons raw honey (liquid or crystallized) or coconut nectar
2   tablespoons lucuma powder
1   teaspoon vanilla bean powder
½   teaspoon lemon zest
¼   teaspoon sea salt
pinch of nutmeg

blueberry macaroons

Makes about 24 macaroons

⅔ cup blueberries

3 tablespoons banana flakes or ½ ripe banana

⅓ cup pure water (a little less if using fresh banana)

2½ cups coconut flakes, macaroon-cut

⅓ cup Brazil nuts, chopped fine

5 tablespoons sun-dried cane juice crystals or coconut sugar

1 tablespoon lucuma powder

1 teaspoon maca powder

few pinches of sea salt

1 teaspoon lemon juice

Blend blueberries, banana, and water in a high-power blender to make a fruit syrup.

Mix all remaining ingredients with the fruit syrup in a large bowl.

Use a tablespoon or use a small ice cream scoop to make macaroons by compacting the mixture in the scoop and releasing.

Place the macaroons on a dehydrator sheet, and dehydrate at 145° for the first 2 hours, then reduce the temperature to 115° and dehydrate for 8 more hours or overnight until the desired texture is achieved. I like them a little chewy. Store in an airtight container.

chef notes	**alternative flavors**

Use any combination of berries for a deliciously colorful cookie, filled with antioxidants.

Strawberries

Raspberries, blended and strained of seeds

Huckleberries

◀ *Bright purple Blueberry Macaroon batter ready to be scooped into mounds.*

plum and hazelnut cookies

Makes about 16 1-inch balls

1   cup dried plums or other dried
    fruit

¾   cup hazelnuts

1   cup walnuts

2   tablespoons sun-dried cane juice
    crystals or coconut sugar

2   tablespoons raw honey (liquid or
    crystallized) or coconut nectar

1   teaspoon camu camu

1   teaspoon vanilla bean powder

few pinches of sea salt

½   teaspoon cinnamon

Chop the dried plums finely, to help them to distribute evenly in the batter since they are semi-hard (soft dried fruits do not need to be chopped).

Pulse the hazelnuts and the walnuts in a food processor until broken down.

Add the dried plums and all remaining ingredients to the food processor, and mix until combined and sticking together like a loose dough.

Roll into balls or, for bars, line an 8 × 8-inch brownie pan with parchment paper, and press the dough into the pan with your hands, then top with another sheet of parchment paper, and roll a straight-sided glass over the top to evenly compact the dough.

Chill for at least 1 hour, then remove from the pan, place on a cutting board, and cut into squares. Store chilled.

chef notes	**alternative flavors**

Substitute the hazelnuts, dried plums, and camu camu with:

Dried bananas + Brazil nuts + maca powder

Dried figs + almonds + ashwagandha extract powder

Dried mango + macadamia nuts + hibiscus powder

strawberry oat thumbprints

Process the strawberries and the honey in a food processor until mostly smooth.

For the Oat Cookies: Process the walnuts and the oats in a food processor until a fine crumble forms.

Add remaining ingredients to the food processor, and mix until a loose dough forms.

Roll into 1-inch balls, and press an indent in the middle for the jam. Set aside.

Drop 1 teaspoon jam into each cookie.

Place cookies on dehydrator sheets at 145° for a few hours, then reduce the temperature to 115° for 8 more hours or overnight. Or bake in the oven at 275° for 25 minutes.

Remove from dehydrator or oven, and serve. Store in an airtight container.

Makes about 16 cookies

Strawberry Jam

½ cup frozen strawberries

1   teaspoon raw honey (liquid) or coconut nectar

Oat Cookies

1½ cups walnuts

¾ cup gluten-free oats or sprouted oat flour

4   tablespoons raw honey (liquid or crystallized) or coconut nectar

1   tablespoon lucuma powder

1   tablespoon mesquite powder

pinch of nutmeg

pinch of cinnamon

pinch of vanilla

¼ teaspoon Himalayan salt

frostings

Super sweet, pretty, and creamy, frostings are one of a kind when made the raw way. The simplicity of the ingredients brings out flavors with a beautiful visual effect of color. Play with colorful fruits and herbs, mix them with some honey and solid coconut oil, and you have a frosting. The variety of frostings is endless—make the traditional fluffy cream frosting, or experiment with chocolate, fruits, and superfoods. Get creative and go play!

◄ *Dark chocolate frosting*

dark chocolate frosting

Great with any chocolate cookie or nut cookie.

Melt the cacao paste and the coconut oil over a double boiler (see Chef Notes: Using a Double Boiler on page 38).

Remove the bowl from the heat, and place on a small towel or cloth (so it doesn't move while stirring).

Mix in the honey or coconut nectar and the sea salt. Stir in the cinnamon and vanilla bean powder.

Spread over cookies when warm for a glaze, or let set for 1 hour chilled then frost with a pastry bag or a frosting tube.

Makes about ½ cup frosting

¼ cup cacao paste, chopped

2 tablespoons coconut oil

3 tablespoons raw honey, liquid, or coconut nectar

pinch of sea salt

pinch of cinnamon

pinch of vanilla bean powder

white chocolate frosting

Tastes great over any chocolate cookie, such as the Double Chocolate Cookie.

Makes about ½ cup frosting

¼ cup cacao butter, chopped

3 tablespoons coconut oil

3 tablespoons raw honey (liquid or crystallized) or coconut nectar

pinch of nutmeg

pinch of sea salt

Melt the cacao butter and the coconut oil over a double boiler (see Chef Notes: Using a Double Boiler on page 38).

Place all ingredients into a high-power blender, and mix to form a silky-smooth texture.

If a hard frosting is desired, chill for 1 hour or so in a glass bowl before frosting cookies. Or pour straight over the cookies on parchment paper, and chill to set.

vanilla frosting

This is a versatile frosting that can be used with most cookie flavors.

Place all ingredients in a food processor, and mix until combined like a frosting. Do not overmix, as the frosting will separate if too warm. Or mix by hand, by vigorously whipping the coconut oil and coconut butter first, then adding remaining ingredients until fluffy.

Place into a pastry bag or a frosting tube. Decorate immediately after making frosting, or if the frosting becomes partially melted, chill about 10 to 25 minutes until set again, and decorate with pastry tips. Alternatively, simply spread the frosting onto cookies with a butter knife or spoon.

Makes about ½ cup frosting

3   tablespoons coconut oil, solid

2   tablespoons coconut butter, solid

3   tablespoons raw honey, crystallized (white preferred), or coconut nectar

1   teaspoon vanilla bean powder

pinch of Himalayan salt

pomegranate glaze

To enjoy the complex flavors of the pomegranate, use this glaze over simple nut cookies that are cut into shapes.

Makes about ¾ cup glaze

4   tablespoons coconut oil

½   cup pomegranate juice, fresh

1   tablespoon chia seeds

1   teaspoon raw honey (liquid or crystallized) or coconut nectar

Melt coconut oil over a double boiler (see Chef Notes: Using a Double Boiler on page 38), or in a jar set in hot water.

Mix all ingredients in a high-power blender until smooth.

Chill in a bowl for about 30 minutes before using.

huckleberry jam

Use in linzer cookies or on thumbprint cookies.

Mix all ingredients in a food processor until the desired consistency forms.

Remove from food processor and place into a bowl. Let set for a few minutes before using as a jam.

Makes about ¾ cup jam

1 cup huckleberries, fresh or frozen, or other berry

3 tablespoons banana flakes or banana powder, or 2 tablespoons lucuma powder

½ teaspoon vanilla bean powder

cinnamon frosting

Use on walnut, hazelnut, or chocolate flavored cookies.

Makes about ½ cup frosting

3 tablespoons coconut oil

3 tablespoons olive oil

¼ cup banana flakes, or
2 tablespoons lucuma plus
½ fresh banana

1 tablespoon raw honey (liquid or
crystallized) or coconut nectar

1 teaspoon cinnamon powder

pinch of nutmeg

pinch of sea salt

Melt coconut oil in a glass jar placed in hot water, or over a double boiler (see Chef Notes: Using a Double Boiler on page 38).

Blend all ingredients in a high-power blender until emulsified.

Pour into a small bowl and use immediately, or chill for 1 hour and then pipe onto cookies.

preparing the plate:
decorating and artful presentation

Choose a plate that complements the type of cookie you are making. Add a little color if the cookies are brown or white. Edible flowers are a beautiful addition and provide a gourmet touch. Arrange the cookies in a pattern, in a circle or in lines, and stack them if the cookie type permits.

When serving to your family or at a party, spend a little time preparing the decoration to ensure that the arrangement is beautiful. This is the time to use colorful frostings or edible flowers. Dip the cookies in chocolate or drizzle some fruit sauce over the top of each cookie for a unique and yummy touch.

I like to combine different types of cookies on a plate when serving a group, so there is something for everyone. Cookies are easy to make and bite-sized, which is perfect for a party.

resources

Online Stores

Longevity Warehouse, www.longevitywarehouse.com: An online superstore of specialty superfood and herbal ingredients of the highest quality.

Mountain Rose Herbs, www.mountainroseherbs.com: An online shop for organic bulk herbs and spices, my go-to store for tea, herbs, hibiscus powder, and true (sweet) cinnamon.

Brands I Love

Wilderness Poets, www.wildernesspoets.com: My favorite source for nut butters and specialty nuts, all organic, including Hawaiian macadamia nuts, Oregon hazelnuts, and Oregon pumpkin seeds.

Longevity Power, www.longevitypower.com: Find high-quality herbal supplements here, including a great black maca extract called Maca Bliss.

Living Libations, www.livinglibations.com: The best source for high-quality essential oil blends for edible elixirs, skincare, and holistic dentistry by Nadine Artemis.

index

acknowledgments

Special thanks to my friends and family for encouraging this book-making process, and for tasting these delicious and healthy recipes. To my loving husband Brian, who gives me peace of mind and the ability to constantly be creative. To my mom, who always gave me the freedom to play and to make art, with all the right tools. To my dad, who makes me laugh and persevere through the most difficult challenges. To my sister, who always has a positive outlook and an openness to learn. Thank you for being there and never doubting my ability to make new and unique creations.

Big thanks to my recipe testers: Malena Corbett, Lisa Miller, Bethanne Wanamaker, and Jenna Kuczynski.

about the author

Julia Corbett is a superfood dessert alchemist and the owner of Diviana Alchemy. Her love of all things healthfully sweet and beautifully designed comes from a background as a competitive runner, always craving sweet treats, and as a photographer. Being inspired to make edible art is a natural inclination, from her love of nature. Julia lives with her husband Brian and dachshund Persephone in Southern California and is native to Washington State. For more information about her and for new recipes, visit her website, Diviana Alchemy, at www.divianaalchemy.com: an online shop of handmade superfood cookies, herbal honey, specialty superfoods, and much more, including Nectar Bars, I Heart Cacao, and Diviana Chocolate.